Nehemiah
Smile Scripture Studies

Rachel Wirges-Lott

PUBLISHED by PARABLES
Earthly Stories with a Heavenly Meaning

SMILE!!! Scripture Studies: Nehemiah
Rachel Wirges-Lott

Copyright © Rachel Wirges-Lott
November, 2016

Published By Parables
November, 2016

All Rights Reserved. No part of this book may be reproduced or utilized in any form or by any means, electronic or mechanical, including photocopying, recording, or by any information storage and retrieval system, without permission in writing from the author.

Unless otherwise specified Scripture quotations are taken from the authorized version of the King James Bible.

ISBN 978-1-945698-10-1

Printed in the United States of America

Readers should be aware that Internet Web sites offered as citations and/or sources for further information may have been changed or disappeared between the time this was written and when it is read.

Nehemiah
Smile Scripture Studies

Rachel Wirges-Lott

History

Smiley devotionals began in a small café, BJ's market café, of North Little Rock, Arkansas. I've been working at BJ's for the past five years. The devotionals were born out of a desire to share God's Word with my coworkers and customers.

I began by writing a short Scripture at the very bottom of the menu for my co-workers. I began adding a smily saying to the Scripture, like, "Smile Jesus Loves You! Smile if You Love Him too!!!" Then I began adding a short commentary about the verse. Eventually, the short comments grew into a devotional on the back of the menus.

I began each devotional with a smiley face and "!!!" because sets of three are superlatives in Hebrew, and I ended each devotional with "!!!!" because that's just the way I am. It also indicates that Jesus is over and above all superlatives!!!

Curious customers began asking what I was writing. When they found out it was a devotional, some started requesting copies. Others began collecting the devotionals.

I was surprised to learn that my little smiley devotionals were being used in classrooms, at churches, at fellowships, and in a prison ministry too!

More than a few told me that I should consider publishing them, a thing I didn't think possible. However, God had other plans.

My prayer is that these devotionals will help you smile in and for Jesus. If you don't know Him, you can! And if you do, then you'll be smiling forever anyway, so start practicing now!!!!

Behold, as the eyes of servants look unto the hand of their masters, and as the eyes of a maiden unto the hand of her mistress; so our eyes wait upon the LORD our God, until that He hath mercy upon us. Psalm 123:2

Smile??? :)

    The psalmist has looked toward the one whom he worships, the only one who makes worship meaningful. He has looked to God. He not only looked to God, he saw God; and when he saw God, he saw himself as he truly was. He was a sinner, one who had rebelled against God, and he was in need of God's mercy. When one comes to worship God, he should expect to see Him. God doesn't hide; when one looks to, he sees, not with the physical eyes but the spiritual sight through God's Word. Then he will see himself as he is. This needs to and should cause him to humble himself before God who is holy, repent of his sin, and wait upon God's mercy. He can expect this mercy ONLY through what Christ has done. Christ died for his sins and paid their price. Only in Him is there mercy.

    Then the psalmist saw that he was not only a sinner saved by grace alone through faith alone, he was as a servant. As such, he humbled to God's care and provision AND to God's will - whatever God desired. His eyes look, they are fixed, upon God their master. He does nothing without consent of God.

    When we come to worship, we look to and should see God. And we will if we worship God in spirit and truth. Then we most humble ourselves before Him. True worship always involves humility. May we see God as He is and praise Him for His mercy to us!!!!

Dedication

    I dedicate this book to God who can do more with it than ever I can imagine. I thank Him for blessing me with this book and the wonderful family (both physical and spiritual) who encouraged and helped me in so many ways. Thank you my parents, siblings, husband, child, in-laws, co-workers, and friends. This book could not contain all the ways God has used you to help me.

The words of Nehemiah the son of Hachaliah. And it came to pass in the month Chisleu, in the twentieth year, as I was in Shushan the palace, that Hanani, one of my brethren, came, he and certain men of Judah; and I asked them concerning the Jews that had escaped, which were left of the captivity, and concerning Jerusalem. - Nehemiah 1:1-2

Nehemiah. Here was a man who stood before God on behalf of the people; and, he stood before the people on behalf of God. He was a captive Jew born during the time of Jewish captivity to the Persians. Despite being born into and raised in captivity, he lived a comfortable life. He lived in the king's palace and served the king in the enviable, highly-esteemed position as the king's cupbearer. What a life!

Even though he was living a comfortable life, Nehemiah cared about his people who had returned home to Jerusalem. They had been home around 100 years. He did not know them nor did he know Jerusalem. Yet, he cared because they were God's people who had returned to the land which God had given them. He knew who he was - he was a Jew, a child of God, and he knew his home was Jerusalem. He did not let his life of ease and his acceptance into Persian society – in the elevated position of king's cupbearer - cause him to forget who he was.

Nehemiah is a good example for everyone. We today would do well to be like him. We need to have a caring heart and not let our position in life blind us to others around us. Whether we be materially well-off or not, we must be caring for others. Nehemiah could have easily forgotten others, but he did not. He could have easily passed by Hananai and not asked how the others were doing. He was a busy man, but he did not allow his business, his wealth, nor his position in life to excuse him from caring about others. We who are children of God do not need to forget others who are near or far from us. We must remember them. We do not need to let our busy lifestyles bury us to caring for others. It is easy to do, but it should not be done. Christ called all those who have repented of sin and believed in Him to show His love to the world. May we never become too big or too busy to stop and care about each person the way Christ would care for them!!!!

And they said unto me, The remnant that are left of the captivity there in the providence are in great affliction and reproach: the wall of Jerusalem also is broken down, and the gates are burned with fire. And it came to pass, when I heard these words, that I sat down and wept, and mourned certain days, and fasted, and prayed before the God of heaven. - Nehemiah 1:3-4

Here we find that Nehemiah's care was not just surface deep; it was genuine and from the heart. He did not ask merely to be polite. He asked with the expectation and hope of truly finding out how they were. What Nehemiah heard brought him to his knees in sorrow. His heart broke over the travail of his people and their home. He didn't hear it and move on unaffected except for a mention of condolence. Nor did he hear it, mourn for a moment, and move on believing he could do nothing about it. He mourned and fasted for days. Then he did the only, but most certainly the best, thing he could do; Nehemiah prayed to God. He took his burden, his care, to God believing God could and would do something about it.

Is our care surface deep; do we truly care about people or do we ask because it's how to greet them politely? How we respond to them - in and out of their presence - reveals our heart for them. Do we rejoice in their good news and mourn in their bad news? When it's bad, do we let our hearts break or callous? Whatever people are going through in their lives, we should bring it to God in prayer. We should thank Him for the good and ask Him for ways to help in the bad. May we truly care!!!!

And said, I beseech Thee, O LORD God of heaven, the great and terrible God, that keepeth covenant mercy for them that love Him and observe His commandments: let Thine ear now be attentive, and Thine eyes open, that Thou mayest hear the prayer of Thy servant, which I pray before Thee now, day and night, for the children of Israel Thy servants, and confess the sins of the children of Israel, which we have sinned against Thee: both I and my father's house have sinned. - Nehemiah 1:5-6

    Nehemiah became distressed about Israel; however, instead of bearing the burden, he brought it to God. Unlike the Persians around him, he did not pray to the god of so-n-so or to any of the many gods they worshiped. He went to the LORD God of heaven. The only one who should be feared and reverenced because He is God alone.

    Nehemiah began his petition by stating that it was a plea. Then he praised God for who He is. Following that, he remembered what God does and what God requires. God is faithful and blesses those who love Him and prove that love by obedience. In whatever state we may find ourselves, may we always praise and thank God for who He is and what He does for us.

    The plea continued with his expressing his desire for God to do something about Israel. He asked for God to hear and answer favorably, see with mercy and compassion. Israel is God's chosen people, His servants. Nehemiah then confessed their sins; he knew why they were in captivity, they had disobeyed God and were punished by God as He said He would. Nehemiah didn't give God reasons why they were good enough to be helped. He simply and humbly stated who God is, who they were, and then pleaded for mercy. May we pray with such awe and humility, for God loves and hears a contrite one!!!!

We have dealt very corruptly against Thee, and have not kept the commandments, nor statutes, nor the judgments, which Thou commandedest Thy servant Moses. Remember, I beseech Thee, the word that Thou commandedest Thy servant Moses, saying, If ye transgress, I will scatter ye abroad among the nations: But if ye turn unto Me, and keep My commandments, and do them; though there were of you cast out unto the uttermost part of the heaven, yet will I gather them from thence, and will bring them unto the place that I have chosen to set my name there. - Nehemiah 1:7-9

Having confessed who God is and who Israel was in God's sight, Nehemiah confessed the depth their depravity went. They broke their covenant with God to worship only Him, and they went whoring after false gods. They broke God's laws even to the extreme of burning their own innocent children as offerings to false gods- they later even ate their own children! They violated God's judgments by declaring wrong to be right and right to be wrong or just not right from person to person. What they did was sin against God alone; true it affected many, but ultimately it was rebellion against God. It wasn't passable or permissible; it was very corrupt from the core of the heart to the character of the person.

Nehemiah remembered that they were in exile because God said and did punish them for their sin. But he then requested that God would show mercy and act upon/remember his promise to gather and bless those who repented of their sins and believed Him. Nehemiah based his hope and pleas on God's promises knowing that God is the faithful keeper of His Word.

While we may not have done exactly what Israel did against God, as sinners, we are corrupt and rebellious against God. Our only plea is in Christ and His death and resurrection for us. Our only hope is in full repentance of sin and belief in Christ. We can pray and safely base our hopes and life on God's Word. When we guide our lives and prayers by God's Word, we can be sure the will of God will be done, and thus our hopes and prayers will be fulfilled!!!!

Now these are Thy servants and Thy people, whom Thou hast redeemed by Thy great power, and by Thy strong hand. O Lord, I beseech Thee, let now Thine ear be attentive to the prayer of Thy servant, and to the prayer of Thy servants, who desire to fear Thy name: and prosper, I pray Thee, Thy servant this day, and grant him mercy in the sight of this man. For I was the king's cup-bearer. - Nehemiah 1:10-11

Who are we who have repented of sin and believed in Christ? We are God's own: His children, His servants. Having been freed from the bondage of serving sin, is there anything better to be and can there be found any greater pleasure in all the world than in that joy found in the fulfilling of God's desires!?

Nehemiah remembered from where Israel came; He recalled how God delivered a people from tirelessly serving the Egyptians. It was by no might of their own and for no merit of their own. For God's own pleasure and by His own power, He redeemed a people and made them a nation, the nation to witness to the world. Based upon and trusting in this truth, Nehemiah pleaded his case before God.

He added that he and others were not just servants, but those servants who desired to fear God's name. Their delight was to do God's will; they wanted nothing else for they knew there was no satisfaction or success without God. Therefore, when they prayed, it was not to elevate themselves that they asked for God to prosper them but to exalt God alone.

Then Nehemiah asked God to grant him mercy before "this man." He knew in God's sight all men are men, even the king to whom he was referring. God set the king to power, and God wielded the king's heart. So, it was by God's hand that a king would look toward, have mercy, and yield to a cup-bearer, who was a captive Jew and a servant. He prayed for an opportunity and the wisdom during the time to do what God willed, for he was the king's cup-bearer who had the position to do something.

God has delivered His own from the bondage of sin; He redeemed us by His power and for His pleasure alone. May it be our delight to serve Him. Then He will bless us with opportunities to serve Him, places to be, and people to see all for His purposes, all for His glory!!!!

SMILE!!! SCRIPTURE STUDIES: NEHEMIAH

And it came to pass in the month Nisan, in the twentieth year of Artaxerxes the king, that wine was brought before him: and I took up the wine, and gave it unto the king. Now I had not been beforetime sad in his presence. Wherefore the king said unto me, Why is thy countenance sad, seeing thou art not sick? This is nothing else but sorrow of heart. Then I was very afraid, - Nehemiah 2:1-2

    For four months, Nehemiah prayed fervently to God. He knew if anyone could help him and move a king's heart toward his plea, it was God. So, Nehemiah appeared sad before the king. To do this could have sentenced him to death for to be sad before the king was a crime. But Nehemiah did; how else would the king know of his sorrow, and how else would he have the opportunity to tell him.

    God moved the king's heart to have compassion on Nehemiah and instead of ordering him to death, asking him what was wrong. This was very unusual for a king, but God answered Nehemiah's prayers and moved the king's heart to accomplish His purpose for both the king and Nehemiah. They both had their positions by God's hand, and now God was working His purpose through them.

    God hasn't changed. He still hears and answers the prayers of His children, but just because we pray doesn't mean we don't do our part to accomplish His will. We must act in faith and trust God to take care of us and everything else involved. The will of God will be accomplished, but we can be part of it - even if it does terrify us at times! We need to create and take the opportunities God gives us!!!!

And said unto the king, let the king live forever: why should not my countenance be sad, when the city of my fathers' sepulchres lieth waste, and the gates thereof are consumed with fire? Then the king said unto me, For what dost thou make request? So, I prayed to the God of heaven. And I said unto the king, If it please the king, and if thy servant have found favour in thy sight, that thou wouldest send me unto Judah, unto the city of my fathers' sepulchres, that I may build it. And the king said unto me, (the queen also sitting by him,) For how long shall thy journey be? And when wilt thou return? So it pleased the king to send me; and I set him a time.

- Nehemiah 2:3-6

Even though Nehemiah had prayed, believed God was with him to accomplish this task, and even was asked by the king what was wrong, he did not act rashly and just wail his travail. He acted wisely. He began by wishing good to the king. Even then he didn't immediately go into his request; he simply told the reason why he was sorrowful. He appealed to the king's heart by mentioning that it was the burial places of his fathers that were lying wasted - a very important part to ancient (especially pagan) societies.

God moved the king's heart to grant Nehemiah a request. But still Nehemiah spoke wisely and didn't blurt it out. Instead, he prayed again (four months of prayer and another), an example for us to follow. And when the king granted that, Nehemiah laid before him a plan. He was prepared.

We need not only pray for opportunities but prepare for them. Therefore, when they come, we will speak wisely and appropriately. We also need to pray through them. Pray; prepare; and pray!!!!

Moreover I said unto the king, If it please the king, let letters be given me to the governors beyond the river, that they may convey me over 'til I come to Judah; And a letter to Asaph the keeper of the king's forest, that he may give me timber to make beams for the gates of the palace which appertained to the house, and for the wall of the city, and for the house that I shall enter into. And the king granted me, according to the good hand of my God upon me. Then I came to the governors beyond the river, and gave them the king's letters. Now the king had sent captains of the army and horsemen with me. - Nehemiah 2:7-9

Nehemiah had not only set a time, but he also gave thought to the materials needed to accomplish this task. Certain now that God was on his side and moving the king's heart toward His will, Nehemiah continued in his request. He knew he needed papers to prove who he was and what he was commissioned to do, and he knew he needed power of permission to acquire the provisions needed to build. So, he asked the king, and the king did so.

Then Nehemiah took a time to give glory to God. He did not take credit for persuading the king to his cause; he said nothing of himself. All that the king had granted was not done so because of him - nor is credit given to the King! What was done was done solely by the good hand of God upon him. If God had not been for him, good would not have happened. The king even granted Nehemiah a powerful escort which was not even requested! And who else but God could have moved the king to give Nehemiah more than what he requested.

Just as Nehemiah, we need to pray, prepare, and pray some more. It took courage to continue to request, but he did because he knew God was for him. God blessed his request with more than Nehemiah had asked. When we act in faith, God will abundantly bless us too. Then, like Nehemiah, we can praise God from whose hand all good things come!!!!

When Sanballat the Horonite, and Tobiah the servant, the Ammonite, heard of it, it grieved them exceedingly that there was come a man to seek the welfare of the children of Israel. - Nehemiah 2:10

Even though Nehemiah sought only to do his people good, there were governors who were upset by it. They didn't want Israel to prosper because Israel's suffering was good for them. Thus they were exceedingly grieved by Nehemiah's desire to do God's will.

There are Sanballats and Tobiahs in today's world. They are grieved by people's desire to accomplish God's will. If a lost sinner repents of sin and believes in Christ to save him, they are grieved for they lost one who would participate in their sin with them. If a child of God desires - as they all should - to live for God, they are grieved because their sin is revealed by the truth in that life. Satan and his own are always grieved when God's will is done in a believer's life.

When Christ was on Earth, many were glad but also many were grieved by His teaching. Surprisingly, it wasn't those who were thought would be grieved who were grieved. It was the religious of His day, those known for their righteousness and those who were followed as spiritual leaders. They were exceedingly grieved because Christ didn't agree with them but revealed them for who they were: good only on the outside but NOT in the heart where it mattered. This grieved them to the point of loathing and plotting to kill Christ.

How about you? Are you a Sanballat? When God's Word shows you where you are wrong or when you are confronted by another whose life shows yours as wrong, are you grieved to anger or to repentance. Don't be a Sanballat. God ALWAYS wins!!!!

So, I came to Jerusalem, and was there three days. And I arose in the night, I and some few men with me; neither told I any man what my God had put in my heart to do at Jerusalem: neither was there any beast with me, save the beast that I rode upon. And I went out by night by the gate of the valley, even before the dragon well, and to the dung port, and viewed the walls of Jerusalem, which were broken down, and the gates thereof were consumed with fire. Then I went on to the gate of the fountain, and to the king's pool: but there was no place for the beast that was under me to pass. Then went I up in the night by the brook, and viewed the wall, and turned back, and entered by the gate of the valley, and so returned.
- Nehemiah 2:11-15

Having arrived in Jerusalem, Nehemiah decided to rest and think his way through the task before him. He knew God was for him, but he didn't rush headlong into the task lest he find himself overwhelmed and under-qualified. He took time to evaluate the situation. He knew he would need to incorporate and encourage the people toward his calling, so he needed to be able to rightly tell them what they faced. It's hard and foolish to give advice without first knowing the situation. Therefore, he carefully planned for each part of Jerusalem's gate.

Nehemiah went out by night with only a few men and no one else there knowing why. He didn't boast in his purpose, he was humble and unassuming. He merely arrived in Jerusalem; he hadn't accomplished anything yet. Furthermore, enemies were watching. He had to be careful.

Besides helping the people physically by building the wall, Nehemiah also wanted to help them spiritually. Because there was no wall, many Jews were scattered in fear. They aligned, married, and were lead astray to false gods by enemy women and men. Also the worship of God - though the temple had been built for around 70 years - was being neglected by priest and people alike. With walls, the people could gather, live in peace, separate themselves from false gods, and worship God.

Just because we know God is with us doesn't mean we should

rush into what He has for us to do. That could lead to burn-out and or disappointment, especially if you want help. It also doesn't mean we should puff up before or after we perform the task; that could lead to humiliation, and it assuredly doesn't please God. Then we must also consider not just the physical but spiritual needs of people. Both action and advice are best when considered and prayed about first!!!!

SMILE!!! SCRIPTURE STUDIES: NEHEMIAH

And the rulers knew not whither I went, or what I did; neither had I as yet told it to the Jews, nor to the priest, nor to the nobles, nor to the rulers, nor to the rest that did the work. Then said I unto them, Ye see the distress that we are in, how Jerusalem lieth waste, and the gates thereof are burned with fire: come and let us build up the wall of Jerusalem, that we be no more a reproach.   - Nehemiah 2:16-17

    Having gone out to the gates and secretly evaluated them, Nehemiah addressed the people. He did not begin by boasting about himself and what he came to do. In fact, he didn't even mention that God put it in his heart to rebuild or that the king was moved to favor the plan. He did not immediately jump into his purpose for coming. Nehemiah began by pointing out to the people that Israel was in ruins and a reproach. It was shameful to be a Jew in Jerusalem. They were God's chosen people in their God given home and it was a shame! Why? They were the people God loved and wanted; they were where God wanted them to be; why was it a shame; why wasn't God blessing them? They were a shame because they were not doing what God desired of them, thus they were not only spiritually ruined but physically. It takes more to be blessed than being where you're suppose to be - though that is the start. It takes doing what you're supposed to do. You can be the right person at the right place; but if you're not doing what you're meant to do, why are you there, for it's a waste and furthermore more of a shame than if you weren't there at all!

    Now note, this was not a reprimand from Nehemiah. He was simply stating how things were. He was not blaming anyone. Instead, he said "we". Though he wasn't there when they returned, wasn't born there, and had only just arrived, he associated himself with them in distress. He was still a Jew, and thus their shame was his shame too. He wasn't abashing them; he was associating with and admonishing them. He loved them. When we seek to help others, let us not callously command them - though there are times that require us to be harsh and demanding - but let us affectionately admonish them. Let us not forget who we were without Christ and who we are with Him. We are unforgiven and hell-bound without Him and forgiven heaven-bound with Him, but we are still sinners! Sin is a shame no matter in whose life it is, and we are not beyond any sin. Let us be God's people where God wants us doing in humility and love what God wants!!!!

Then I told them of the hand of my God which was good upon me; as also the king's words that he had spoken unto me. And they said, Let us rise up and build. So they strengthened their hands for this good work.
- Nehemiah 2:18

He told them of his purpose and his plan, now Nehemiah told Israel of the person behind the purpose. He did not point to himself claiming that he alone planned and would do this. Nor did he give glory to the king though the king was who commissioned and sent him. Nehemiah focused on and glorified God. He recognized that all good things ultimately come from the hand of God, and that it was only by God's grace that he had come so far. As further proof of God's grace and His pleasure in the work, he told of the king's words and permission. God wanted this wall built and provided all that was needed to get the job done.

The people then gladly and immediately began to work. They had the grace of God, permission of the king, materials needed, and the leadership of Nehemiah. They were stirred toward the cause. Why, however, had no one tried before Nehemiah to build the wall? They knew it needed to be built. No one tried because no one cared enough; they were either lazy toward it or fearful of it. No one wanted to lead, but everyone was eager to follow and work. So, Nehemiah took on the leadership role and stirred the people to action.

When we see a need, let's not shrink back from doing it. Instead, let's do our best to help. If God lays it on our hearts to do something, let's not be lazy towards it by being busy doing other things. Israel left what God was calling them to do to someone else. We shouldn't do that. And again, we should not be fearful about what God has called us to do either. Fear leads to worry. We worry about how qualified we are. God despises laziness in regards to our doing His will, and He won't bless the work we're doing trying to avoid His will for us. And we should never fear if God calls us to do something, for He will qualify us. It'll take work - just as they had to rise up and strengthen their hands for the work. God won't pour the abilities into us, but He will provide them for us. Then let us at all times stir one another up toward God's work. Whether we lead or follow let us encourage one another in love. And the best way to do this is to recall and tell the wonderful things God has done for us!!!!

> *But when Sanballat the Horonite, and Tobiah the servant, the Ammonite, and Geshem the Arabian, heard it, they laughed us to scorn, and despised us, and said, What is this thing that ye do? Will ye rebel against the king?* - Nehemiah 2:19

Israel began building the wall but not without opposition. Their enemies were long time enemies - century old enemies - a Moabite and an Ammonite. They were grieved exceedingly when they heard of Nehemiah's seeking Israel's welfare. Now Israel was actually doing something! They couldn't physically prevent Israel's building lest they upset the king, so they did something they could. They made fun of them. Though truly fearful and cringing inside, they laughed and mocked Israel's work; they despised them. They mocked their purpose of building the wall by constantly questioning the rational of the project. "What is this thing that ye do?" They lied about their purpose asking, "Will ye rebel against the king?" They tried to stop the work by casting discouragement and fear into Israel's hearts.

Satan and those who reject Christ are no different than Sanballat, Tobiah, and Geshem. They grieve exceedingly when one repents of his sin and believes in Christ, but they fear and cringe when that one begins to live for Christ. Knowing a child of God is eternally secure in Christ, they thus try to cause havoc in his life, cause him to waste his life. Their most effective methods are doubt and fear. Like with Eve, they begin little, "did God REALLY say that; are you sure?" Then they go further, "Well, that's not what He meant." They twist the truth to achieve their own means. Sadly, many believers begin to believe God is rejecting them because things are not as they think they should be. Then they grow disappointed (God isn't blessing me), doubtful (I guess He doesn't love me or mean what He says), and finally bitter (well if that's it, then I'll live as I want and forget God). Doubt can also lead to fear, and fear paralyzes a believer from action. Don't doubt but face fear! God cannot lie; His word is ALWAYS true - know it; believe it. God conquered Satan and sin. Why fear when He is omnipotent!? Have faith in God. Faith dispels doubt and forges past fear!!!!

Then answered I them, and said unto them, The God of heaven, He will prosper us; therefore we His servants will arise and build: but ye have no portion, nor right, nor memorial, in Jerusalem.

- Nehemiah 2:20

How should one deal with discouragement, doubt, and fear? Whether it comes from without or within, these are easy to fall prey. Then they wreak havoc on the life of a believer. The only and best way to handle discouragement, doubt, and fear is to hand it over to God. But how does one do that? He prays, studies the Bible, and remembers what God has already done for Him. Then with the greatest confidence, he can face his problems.

Israel faced terrible mockery and discouragement. The enemy tried to misrepresent their purpose, but Nehemiah combated them wisely. He had prayed about this building of the wall for months. He had prayed to the God of heaven and praised Him for prospering the work thus far. He knew God wanted to bless His people, but he also remembered that God wouldn't bless them if they were in disobedience. He knew God's Word/promises; he fervently prayed and knew God had put this in his heart to do; and he recalled how the hand of God was good upon them. Knowing this, he boldly proclaimed the power and prosperity of God and thus their resolve as His servants to accomplish His will. They had faith that God would see them through this and deliver them.

Nehemiah then told the enemies their condemnation. Because they despised and discouraged the work of God, they would have no part and no right to claim a part in their prosperity from God. Furthermore, their efforts would be futile. They did not belong in Jerusalem, and they would not even be remembered in Jerusalem. Children of the world, rejecters of Christ, have no part in or claim to the blessings God gives His own. Belong to Christ, do His will, and He will prosper you for the glory of God!!!!

Then Eliashib the high priest rose up with his brethren the priest, and they builded the sheep gate; and they sanctified it, and set up the doors of it; even to the tower of Meah they sanctified it, unto the tower of Hananeel. - Nehemiah 3:1

Israel did not just say they were going to work and prepare for it, they began to work! Nehemiah stirred them to work, and they worked. Each family worked on the gate section closest to his home. Each had his own personal reason - to protect his family - but each also worked toward the good of the whole - protection of their nation. These people, however, were not naturally builders; their trade was herding and farming. But still they worked as they could and as God had desired them to do. They said and did their work.

The first family mentioned is the Levites. These were they who were called and set apart to be priest for Israel; they were mediators between God and Israel. The people by sacrifices and taxes provided all the priest needed. The high priest Eliashib was the only one to meet directly with God; he did this once a year on the Day of Atonement when he entered the Holies of Holies where the Mercy Seat was. There he made a sacrifice for the entire nation.

The priest - and especially the high priest - could have easily thought themselves too good for this work. But they didn't; no one is too good to work for God but everyone should join in the work. They could have claimed that the people should build the walls around the temple and take care of them. Again they did not. They refused to shirk the work to another. It was God's work and thus their work. They followed Nehemiah's leadership thus encouraging the people to do likewise. They worked as one of the common men. They led the people by example, built, and sanctified the work and wall for God. May we lead by example and not merely speak, but work for the Lord!!!!

And next to him builded the men of Jericho. And next to them builded Zaccur the son of Imri. - Nehemiah 3:2

"The men of Jericho": here Nehemiah mentions one of the three neighboring cities that helped build the wall. The men of Jericho returned with Ezra and the first returnees, but they did not live in Jerusalem. This, however, did not hinder them from building the wall with and for their brothers and neighbors. The well-fare of their fellow brothers concerned them, and thus their brother's prosperity was also a blessing to them though it was to no advancement of their own city. They acted out of a genuine love. They rode and walked miles just to help build Jerusalem's walls.

When we see our fellow brothers and sisters in Christ in need of help in their work for God, what do we do? Do we think we have not the time to help them because we are busy with our own lives and problems? Do we turn away believing it is not our responsibility? Do we try to ignore them so we won't be held accountable for not helping or try to avoid them so we won't be asked? All these are, sadly, common responses, but they should not be. If there is a need and a way we can fulfill it, we should go the extra mile and help. We should do it not for glory, but out of a genuine love. Their prosperity in God's work should delight and encourage us. And above all, we must act with a Christ-like love. He came and He gave His all for us. His life, suffering, sacrifice for our sin, and resurrection was all for us and the honor and glory of God. Our salvation was His joy, His reason for enduring our cross. God Himself rejoices when one repents of sin and believes in Christ.

May we seek ways to help in God's work, and may we help with a Christian love!!!!

> *But the fish gate did the sons of Hassenaah build, who also laid the beams thereof, and set up the doors thereof, the locks thereof, and the bars thereof. And next to them repaired Meremonth the son of Urijah, the son of Koz. And next unto them repaired Meshullam the son of Berechiah, the son of Meshezabeel. And next unto them repaired Zadok the son of Baana. And next unto them the Tekoites repaired; but their nobles put not their necks to the work of the Lord.* - Nehemiah 3:3-5

  There was much work to do on not just the whole wall but every gate and every part of the wall. There were rocks and mortar to be laid, beams and bars to raise, doors and locks to set. Thankfully, many families joined together under Nehemiah's leadership and put their "necks to the work of their Lord." They built up the gates, repaired the walls, and encouraged each other in the work. And everyone was important to their task at hand.

  Not everyone, however, and sadly, joined in the work of their Lord. The nobles of the Tekoites refused to help despite their people more than eagerly worked on their section of the wall and then some! They "put not their necks to the work of their Lord." Literally this Hebrew idiom means, they did not submit to the work. Though they had the responsibility and the capability, they did not have reliability. They were as a stubborn mule that refuses to move although the field is before him, the yolk is upon him, and the leadership is behind him. Stupid, useless: these are words best suited for them. Does it matter their reason? No. If they did not like Nehemiah, they did not like the man of the Lord meaning they thought themselves better than the Lord, for they could have chosen better. If they thought themselves above such work, they thought themselves above God's work. There is none above ANY work God gives him to do for no one is master of God. God puts us in positions to do His will; we might as well not be there if we don't work for Him! These men were nobles by name but not by deed. If anyone should have worked, it should have been them. May we ALWAYS work for God!!!!

Moreover the old gate repaired Jehoiada, the son of Paseah, and Meshullam the son of Besodeiah; they laid the beams thereof, and set up the doors thereof, and the locks thereof, and the bars thereof. And next unto them repaird Melatiah the Gibeonite, the men of Bigeon, and Mizpah, unto the throne of the governor on this side of the river. - Nehemiah 3:6-7

Opposite to the previously mentioned nobles of the Tekoites, the family of Jehoiada and the family of Meshullam joined forces and worked. Each one too small to build the gate on their own, they worked together on it. Neither was too proud to accept the other's help when Nehemiah put them together to work. Only by working together and in harmony were they able to complete the gate. At times, we may need help. Though others may be doing great things on their own, we may need to join with another to do God's will. This is no shame but a blessing for both people involved. May we never hesitate not only to help but to be helped when we need it that we may not miss the things two can do for God together!

Then we have the people from Gibeon and Mispah coming to help. The Gibeonites dressed in rags, claimed to be from far away, and tricked Israel into sparing their lives and making them slaves. That was centuries ago. Since then, Israel had been enslaved for 70 years and released. Now, they came 8 miles to help Israel build their walls! Then men of Mizpah came 5 miles to help build. They repaired to the throne of the governor. Again two joined and accomplished what one could not. Work together; accomplish a lot!!!!

Next unto them repaired Uzziel the son of Harhalah, of the goldsmiths. Next unto him also repaired Hananiah the son of one of the apothecaries, and they fortified Jerusalem unto the broad wall. And next unto them repaired Rephaiah the son of Hur, the ruler of the half part of Jerusalem. - Nehemiah 3:8-9

Here are two men who could have said "I can't." Yet Uzziel the goldsmith and Hananiah the apothecary said instead "I can." They were not skilled builders nor did they have experience in the field, but that did not stop them. When God called to rebuild the wall, they answered. God will and can use those who are willing to work for Him. There are only two requirements that one must have to work for God. The first and most important is salvation. If one has not turned from his sin to God and believed that Christ died and rose again to save him, then he cannot work for God. He may claim and even believe he is working for God, but he is not and cannot be if he hasn't repented of sin and believed in Christ. Why? He is still in his sin. God says that apart from Christ all our righteousness is vile and disgusting rags tossed before Him. Without Christ, we can do NOTHING for God!

The next requirement is willingness. What God can do through a willing child of His is endless. Since God qualifies whom He calls, there is no need to say "I can't" when He desires a work from you.

Uzziel and Hanaiah said "I can" and they did through and for God. And next unto them was Rephaiah the ruler. This man could have used his title to excuse himself, but he didn't. He followed the priest's example and worked. He said "I will." When it comes to God's work, let us always say "I can and I will" and let God work through us!!!!

And next unto them repaired Jedaiah the son of Harumaph, even over against his house. And next unto him repaired Hattush the son of Hashabniah. Malchijah the son of Harim, and Hashub the son of Pahathmoab, repaired the piece, and the tower of the furnaces. - Nehemiah 3:10-11

Here we find more willing workers. Each willing worker works for his own benefit and at the same time he works for the benefit of the whole. Jedaiah, Hattush, and Hashub: this may be the only place in the entire Bible these men are mentioned, but what a place! They are noted by God in His eternal Word for merely building the wall God desired for them to build. What an honor, not only did they benefit their own families and nation, but they were eternally recorded for doing such. It was plainly logical to build the wall; it was nothing new for a city to build a wall, and yet what honor each individual who helped received!

Malchijah is mentioned earlier in scripture, but it wasn't such an honorable note. Malchijah was one who had directly disobeyed God (Ezra 10:31). When the second leader Ezra returned many years earlier, Malchijah angered him by marrying a pagan woman. Here, he has repented and is working heartily for God. God honors him with the rest of the workers for his work.

We may think, now, it is such a great honor to be in the Bible for just doing God's will - especially since it was so logical! We may further think that Malchijah should not have received so equal honor as the rest. God, however, is the same way, in that He is gracious to us. We sin against Him daily, yet He forgives; and instead of marking our sins, He remembers our works for Him that He may reward us with eternal rewards! Remember, hope, and work in this truth!!!!

And next unto him repaired Shallum the son of Halohesh, the ruler of the half part of Jerusalem, he and his daughters. The valley gate repaired Hanun, and the inhabitants of Zanoah; they built it, and set up the doors thereof, the locks thereof, and the bars thereof, and a thousand cubits on the wall unto the dung gate. - Nehemiah 3:12-13

In a society where the role and pride of women were to marry and have children, we find the daughters of Shalhum working on the wall with their father! Their father, however, was no ordinary man but a ruler of half of Jerusalem. No doubt he could have and did summon up his servants to work, but his daughters wanted to help anyway. They didn't have to work; they were not expected to help - in fact they may have been discouraged against it; they could have easily sat out, but they did not. When God called for Israel to build the wall, they answered. They knew that God wanted them to build with their people.

In our society, what is wrong is proclaimed right or at least acceptable and what is right is deemed as wrong, bigotry, hatred, and etc... It is easy for a child of God to follow along with the world, compromise the truth to fit in, and make exceptions and excuses not to do as God calls for him to do. Society expects this of us and desires that we fit in with them. God, however, has called us to work, and we aren't expected to do it by using the world's ways. God, who judges, has called us, and HE expects us to obey. He is the one who matters; if none else but He expects us to do something, then we had still better quickly and happily do it.

Then as The inhabitants of Zanoah of Judah, we had better not just do what is required, but more so if able. They repaired 1,500 feet they didn't have to repair! May we not only do the unexpected, but exceed it when God calls and enables us!!!!

But it came to pass, that when Sanballat heard that we builded the wall, he was wroth, and took great indignation, and mocked the Jews. And he spake before his brethren and the army of Samaria, and said, What do these feeble Jews? Will they fortify themselves? Will they sacrifice? Will they make an end in a day? Will they revive the stones out of the heaps of the rubbish which are burned? Now Tobiah the Ammonite was by him, and he said, Even that which they build, if a fox go up, he shall even break down their stone wall.   - Nehemiah 4:1-3

    Israel began building the wall, and their enemies began taunting them even greater than earlier. This time, Sanballat spoke not only to a few but to his brethren and his entire Samaritan army! He scorned, abashed, and disparaged the Jews and their wall in front of hundreds of people. Then Tobiah joined in the "fun." Satan always discredits the work of God, and he calls on his armies of demons to do the same; and the world of his own follow suit. All their attempts, however, are futile for Christ has already defeated them. He did so by His sinless life and perfect, willing sacrifice of Himself on our cross and His resurrection from the dead. He bore ALL sin-and He's omniscience so He knew every sin - and God's wrath upon it. He did so that we may not have to do it. If there was one sin He didn't bear, then He didn't conquer it and He couldn't forgive man and give eternal life with God. But He did and He can. Thus, the worst thing anyone in Hell has done is reject Christ for it alone is why they are there. The best thing anyone in heaven has done is accept Christ's completed work for that alone is why they are there. Christ totally conquered Satan and sin so we need never listen to their slanders when we are working for God because He will accomplish His work through us!!!!

Hear, O our God; for we are despised: and turn their reproach upon their own head, and give them for a prey in the land of captivity: And cover not their iniquity, and let not their sin be blotted out from before Thee: for they have provoke Thee to anger before the builders. - Nehemiah 4:4-5

The best way to deal with any problems or troubles is to immediately call upon God. God's ears are always open to the cries and pleas of His own and to the repentant believing prayer of one coming to Him for salvation. Therefore, we can always be sure God hears us. We can also be sure that He listens to us and always does what is best for us that we may be more Christ-like in our lives.

So, when - not if - the world despises us, we can cry to God. The reproach of the world upon us will become their reproach when Christ returns and judges this world. They will see and know that the Bible and its believers are right, but it will be too late. What they desired upon God's own will be their end instead. Their sin of disbelief in Christ will condemn them. It will not be covered by the blood of Christ; they are unforgiven but by their own choice.

Then will God's wrath be poured out upon all sin. The time for mercy will be done. This day is coming without delay: every moment draws it closer to the present.

Who is on the Lord's side and who belongs to Satan? Who is working for the Lord accomplishing His desires and who is fulfilling death in their own bodies? No one needs be on Satan's side. Whosoever can repent of sin and believe in Christ. Then they can overcome any problem by calling on God who will accomplish His will through them!!!!

So built we the wall; and all the wall was joined together unto the half thereof: for the people had a mind to work. - Nehemiah 4:6

Once Nehemiah and possibly the workers finished praying, they continued working. They did not sit back and wait for their enemies and problems to vanish before they continued working. They did not try to bribe or bargain with God to rid them of their problems, nor did they attempt to excuse their work because of their problems. They prayed and worked knowing with confidence that God would care for them who were doing His will.

God hasn't changed; He will still protect and provide for those doing His work. Paul wrote in 2 Corinthians 4:8-9, "We are troubled on every side, yet not distressed; we are perplexed but not in despair; persecuted, but not forsaken: cast down, but not destroyed," and 12:9, "My grace is sufficient for thee: for my strength is made perfect in weakness." Therefore, let us work! When troubles come, let us pray and work on! Let us never-ever excuse our work for God because of our problems, but let us work to and through them without halting or faltering. God is with us working in and through us toward His glorious purpose. If God be for us, who can stand against us?! Why should we worry what mere man can do to us?! Work on! There will not ever be a moment God has nothing for you to do, so we had better get doing for God.

"And the wall was joined together....for the people had a mind to work." Literally, they had a heart to work. One can put his back into it without his heart, but he cannot put his heart into it without his back. Do all things heartily, as unto the Lord and not men. Let us not just put effort but heart into God's work lest it be for nothing!!!!

But it came to pass that when Sanballat, and Tobiah, and the Arabians, and the Ammonites, and the Ashdodites heard that the walls of Jerusalem were made up, and that the breaches began to be stopped, then they were very wroth. And conspired all of them together to come and fight against Jerusalem, and to hinder it. Nevertheless we made our prayer unto our God, and set a watch against them day and night, because of them.
- Nehemiah 4:7-9

Nehemiah and Israel prayed; but instead of getting relief from their trouble, they got more trouble! In fact, it got a lot worse. Now there were many more joined together by their hate and conspiring against Israel who had done nothing to them. They were all angry only because Israel was building its wall. They were so angry they plotted to fight them so the wall wouldn't be built.

Israel was small beside them; it was three groups of people against one! Physically it seemed hopeless. However, Israel knew they were not working on their own might but God's power. They prayed once again and set up a watch against the enemies. They trusted God to care for them, so they did their part and set a watch.

In today's world, a believer is beset on every hand by those people and things - whether physical or other - that would hinder him. At times people attempt to lead him astray from those things he should be doing or from the person he should be. Other times, things (prosperity, power, popularity) draw him with their strings and make him their puppet. And still yet, at times and sadly, he allows himself to draw himself away. These enticements may not be bad (acceptance, health, life), but when they become a believer's focus, they become a believer's sin. Thus, let us set up a watch against anyone or thing that may hinder our work for God, and let us be ready to resist by God's Word those that would have us quit God's work!!!!

SMILE!!! SCRIPTURE STUDIES: NEHEMIAH

And Judah said, the strength of the bearers of burdens is decayed, and there is much rubbish; so that we are not able to build the wall.
- Nehemiah 4:10

Enemies beset them; they worked night and day at a job to which they were not accustomed; rubbish made things even more difficult: when it rains, it pours as some say. With everything going wrong though they were doing right, one can easily sympathize with Judah. They were tired, however, one shouldn't agree with them. They were excusing themselves from doing God's work; they were focused on the situation rather than the Sustainer; they were complying with their enemies' desires. This makes them wrong in their complaining and desiring to quit.

Many today, sadly, see things as Judah saw their situation. They try their best to do all things God desires of them, but troubles come. For a while they endure and press on encouraging themselves; but as troubles grow greater and the work becomes harder, they begin to complain, then excuse themselves, and finally quit. It happens so often. Jesus spoke about it in the parable of the sower. His Word fell on a stony ground, grew, but died: this was a person's heart. They heard the Word, with great joy began to work, but when troubles and persecution arose, they wanted to quit. Many do.

So, how can we avoid this tragedy? Instead of focusing on our situation, we must focus on our Sustainer. Our Sustainer is not only our purpose for working but our power for working. We must fill our lives with His Word. Therefore, when troubles come, the Holy Spirit can recall to our minds His Word, and we can use it to bear the troubles and resist the temptation to complain and quit. Let us focus on God and do all things without murmuring and complaining but unto God!!!!

And our adversaries said, They shall not know, neither see, till we come in the midst among them, and slay them, and cause the work to cease. And it came to pass, that when the Jews which dwelt by them came, they said unto us ten times, From all places whence ye shall return unto us they will be upon you. Therefore, set I in the lower places behind the wall, and on the higher places, I even set the people after their families with their swords, their spears, and their bows. And I looked, and rose up, and said unto the nobles, and the rulers, and to the rest of the people, Be not ye afraid of them: remember the Lord which is great and terrible, and fight for your brethren, your sons, and your daughters, your wives, and your houses.

– Nehemiah 4:11-14

It was during their mid-work crisis, their time of weakness and depression that the enemy decided to plot and act against Israel. They believed that they were doing so in secret, but they were wrong. God was watching them and warning His people, even though Israel was complaining at the time. God not only knew the plan they made, He knew the plan before they made it! He had it all under control. He had Jews in place to hear and warn their brethren. Upon hearing the news, Nehemiah didn't despair. He simply set up a fortified watch and then encouraged them to stay strong.

The words Nehemiah spoke were words God spoke to encourage His leaders and prophets when they were surrounded by trouble, "Be not afraid: remember the Lord which is great and terrible." Nehemiah did not say to rely on their own walls or strength of men but to remember (act upon the truth of) the Lord. Numerous times God assures us that He is there and not to be afraid. What peace we can have if we would only trust Him.

It is normally when we are most down that our enemies attack. Complaining helps the foe. Depression and pity strike first, and then comes anger, maybe fear and finally apathy. Those are some; our other enemies include: Satan, the world, and physical enemies. But when our enemies gather around us and plot against us, let us remember first that

God already knows and controls the entire situation and will take care of us. Then let us also remember to continue to do what God desires us to do and stop complaining while we are at it! And let us draw our courage and strength from remembering the Lord, who He is, what He has done, and what He promises to do!!!!

And it came to pass, when our enemies heard that it was known unto us, and God had brought their counsel to naught, that we returned all of us to the wall, everyone unto his work. And it came to pass from that time forth, the half of my servants wrought in the work, and the other half held both the spears, the shields, and the bows, and the habergeons; and the rulers were behind all the house of Judah. They which builded the wall, and they that bear burdens, with those that laded, everyone with one of his hands wrought the work, and with the other hand held a weapon. For the builders, every one had his sword girded by his side, and so builded. And he that sounded the trumpet was by me. - Nehemiah 4:15-18

Though hand joins in hand, those who oppose the Lord will surely fall. The enemies' plots to attack and cause the work to cease failed without even a finger lifted. God had seen to it; it was prevented. All their plans came to nothing because God sent someone to warn Israel and allow them to prepare. Then having lost the advantage of secrecy, the enemy decided not to attack. And who did they hear brought their counsel to naught but God himself. Whether they believed it or not, they heard that God was for Israel.

Then Nehemiah had everyone return to work but this time with a sword on hand ready at a moment's notice to fight. He had half the people armored and watching over the work and the rest with sword but working. And as he supervised the wall, a trumpeter followed him prepared to be the alarm if needed.

Though Nehemiah knew God was with them, he still was fully ready to fight, but he didn't stop the work and wait for it. God's own may not face physical battles, but we do face spiritual battles everyday. With God, we can win. This doesn't, however, mean we don't prepare to fight. God isn't going to help us if we don't ready ourselves with His Word. We also should continue work; why fight to work and not work!? Be ready, but continue working or you've already lost!!!!

And I said unto the nobles, and to the rulers, and to the rest of the people, the work is great and large, and we are separated upon the wall, one from another. In what place therefore ye hear the sound of the trumpet, resort ye thither unto us: our God shall fight for us. So we laboured in the work: and half of them held the spears from the rising of the morning till the stars appeared. Likewise at the same time said I unto the people, let every one with his servant lodge within Jerusalem, that in the night they may be a guard to us, and labour on the day. So neither I, nor my brethren, nor my servants, nor the men of the guard which followed me, none of us put off our clothes, saving that every one put them off for washing.

- Nehemiah 4:19-23

Nehemiah encouraged the people, from the greatest to least. He didn't deny reality by saying it would get easier or that the enemy wouldn't be threatening to attack, but he did devise a plan. He admitted the work was hard and of great extent. Then he presented the problem: the wall was so long that many were left alone on their part of it. The enemy could attack them causing great harm and hurt. Then he proposed a plan: when the trumpet sounded, the people were to rush to it and fight. Lastly, but most encouraging he praised the Protector. He did not say they must fight alone, but that God would fight for them. This meant though they may need to battle, God would ensure their victory! They didn't have to worry about it, just do what God wanted. What encouragement!

This, however, wasn't a lighter work load time. It got even more strenuous. Guards watched, and people worked ALL day. At night for protection, they dwelt in Jerusalem. And for readiness, they wore their clothes at all times except washing. And Nehemiah worked too.

Many today try to encourage but by sugar-coating circumstances. This isn't only lying but actually making the problem worse! Why? It presents a false "reality" or hope and will leave one worse off. The best encouragement comes not from denying problems but from depending on God and then continuing His work. Christ's death and resurrection conquered sin. Trust in and be encouraged by that. Then work on!!!!

And there was a great cry of the people and of their wives against their brethren the Jews. For there were that said, We, our sons, and our daughters, are many: therefore we take up corn for them, that we may eat, and live. Some also there were that said, We have mortgaged our lands, vineyards, and houses, that we might buy corn, because of the dearth. There were also that said, We have borrowed money for the king's tribute, and that upon our lands and vineyards. Yet now our flesh is as the flesh of our brethren, our children as their children: and, lo, we bring into bondage our sons and our daughters to be servants, and some of our daughters are brought into bondage already: and neither is it in our power to redeem; for other men have our land and vineyards. - Nehemiah 5:1-5

Not only were there problems from the enemies outside but from the brethren inside Israel! Everyone was busy building and doing what God desired. This, however, didn't mean they didn't need food, or that their bills were paid for them. On top of that, a great shortage of crop made it impossible for them to pay their bills AND eat! So, their great families went hungry. Many were destitute and in debt. What made this worse was that their fellow brethren took advantage of them in their sad condition. The people sold houses and lands to buy food and pay bills; but then without a way to grow food and earn money, they eventually sold themselves into slavery to their richer brethren. This was wrong of their brethren to exploit them, but yet it happened.

Sadly, the people of God don't always act as they should. Instead of trying to make a situation better, they make it worse. This was the case when the apostles tried to hush a blind man who was calling out to Jesus. This is the case when a child of God finds one in a bad situation (maybe by his own doing) and gloats, talks badly to and about them, does something "nice" but for something in return, or just simply walks away and does nothing at all. Christ could have done all these things when we rebelled against Him and condemned ourselves to eternal torment in Hell, but He didn't. He came and took our punishment of death that we all by repentance and belief would be forgiven and live eternally with God. We can't repay Him, yet He came. Don't make the bad worse; love as Christ loved and truly help those in need!!!!

And I was very angry when I heard their cry and these words. Then I consulted with myself, and I rebuked the nobles, and the rulers, and said unto them, Ye exact usury, every one of his brother. And I set a great assembly against them. And I said unto them, We after our ability have redeemed our brethren the Jews, which were sold unto the heathen; and will ye even sell your brethren? Or shall they be sold unto us? Then held they their peace, and found nothing to answer. Also I said, It is not good that ye do: ought ye not to walk in the fear of our God because of the reproach of the heathen our enemies? I likewise, and my brethren, and my servants, might exact from them corn: I pray you, let us leave off this usury. Restore, I pray you, to them, even this day, their lands, their vineyards, their olive yards, and their houses, also the hundredth part of the money, and of the corn, the wine, and the oil, that ye exact of them. - Nehemiah 5:6-11

Naturally, Nehemiah was angry when he heard how his own people were cruelly treated by each other, and they were supposed to be helping one another! Rather than madly storming himself over to the nobles and rulers, however, he paused and thought - and probably prayed too. This is a good idea for everyone. Don't act in anger because it is so easy to enrage ourselves to sin. Pause and think about things, the best ways to handle it.

Then Nehemiah called them to a meeting, a great assembly of accusers. He spoke reminding them of how God had brought them out of bondage, and then questioned why should they then be cruelly mistreating and enslaving the poor. They were silently shameful - and what really could they say being wrong! Nehemiah continued and condemned their acts because it was against God's law. He didn't stop there though; He didn't reveal the sin without responding with a solution, and not just a solution but an example which he and his set forth. He loaned without usury and told them to do the same and restore the properties of the poor. When we find a problem, we should not be so quick to reveal it without first having a solution; and if it's in one's actions, an example in ourselves for them to follow. Bring it to the Bible, and live the example!!!!

Then they said, We will restore them, and will require nothing of them; so will we do as thou sayest. Then I called the priest, and took an oath of them, that they should do according to this promise. Also I shook my lap, and said, So God shake out every man from his house, and from his labour, that performeth not this promise, even thus be he shaken out, and emptied. And all the congregation said, A-men, and praised the LORD. And the people did according to this promise. - Nehemiah 5:12-13

    The best thing a person can do when confronted with their sin is repent and do what is right. The people had broken God's law, confessed - by silence - their guilt, repented, and now desired to make restitution to those whom they wronged.

    Nehemiah made them promise to fulfill their word and then pronounced a curse upon any who did not do as they promised. He shook the folds of his robe out - or rather emptied his pockets for that's what folds were - as a symbol of what would happen to those who refused to do as they said. He said they would be "shaken out of" their houses and jobs – and then, they would be left with nothing. Truly, this is the end of all those who acquire riches by deceit and fraud, the end of those who hoard riches unto themselves. They lose everything.

    The people answered "Amen", let it be so. Then they praised the Lord in worship to Him. Following that, they did fulfill their oaths.

    When we sin, we must not only repent but make restitution to those whom we wronged. At times this is as simple as a sorry; other times it takes more; and at all times it takes sacrifice of self. Restoring fellowship between you and one wronged is not always easy and takes time, patience, and sacrifice. But it is always worth it, for those who do not try are not only out of fellowship with the one but with God and thus will not be as blessed as he could be!!!!

Moreover from the time that I was appointed to be their governor in the land of Judah, from the twentieth year even unto the two and thirtieth year of Artaxerxes the king, that is, twelve years, I and my brethren have not eaten the bread of the governor. But the former governors that had been before me were chargeable unto the people, and had taken of them bread and wine, beside forty shekels of silver; yea, even their servants bare rule over the people: but so did not I, because of the fear of God. Yea, also I continued in the work of this wall, neither bought we any land: and all my servants were gathered thither unto the work. Moreover there were at my table an hundred and fifty of the Jews and rulers, beside those that came unto us from among the heathen that are about us. Now that which was prepared for me daily was one ox and six choice sheep; also fowls were prepared for me, and once in ten days store of all sorts of wine: yet for all this required not I the bread of the governor, because the bondage was heavy upon this people. Think upon me, my God, for good, according to all that I have done for this people. - Nehemiah 5:14-19

Nehemiah and his men spent 12 years in Judah, and not one time did they eat the food of the governor. This was because he knew the governor would take from the people. The poor people had already given and owed so much they were even lower than the servants! Nehemiah wanted to help the people, thus he had no part - not even the slightest - in causing them grief. He not only avoided taxing and robbing them, but he also worked on the wall with them, charged them nothing, fed many workers, and cared for them. He truly loved his people.

Then he prayed that God would deal kindly with him in his life as he had dealt kindly to the people. He wanted to reap what he sowed. He wanted God's blessings.

When we truly care for people, we will not only avoid causing them grief directly, but also be careful not to do it indirectly. We will give what we can without expecting payment; we will come alongside them and do what we can to encourage them in the Lord. Then we can rest assured that God will bless us. It may not be materially and may not be even on earth, but He will bless and reward EVERY work done for Him!!!!

Now it came to pass when Sanballat, and Tobiah, and Geshem the Arabian, and the rest of our enemies, heard that I had builded the wall, and that there was no breach left therein; (though at that time I had not set up the doors upon the gates;) that Sanballat and Geshem sent unto me, saying, Come, let us meet together in some one of the villages in the plain of Ono. But they thought to do me mischief. And I sent messengers unto them, saying, I am doing a great work, so that I cannot come down: why should the work cease, whilst I leave it, and come down to you? Yet they sent unto me four times after this sort; and I answered them after the same manner.
- Nehemiah 6:1-4

We may believe Nehemiah would have to be very foolish to accept an invitation to meet with his enemies, especially since they wanted to do him harm. However, they were saying it was in the name of peace and reconciliation. Nehemiah knew their lie because he knew the persecution they had already afflicted upon them and that they really had not changed. So he replied that he was busy with God's work and to meet with them would mean the work would stop which was what they wanted all along. Despite the enemy's persistence, Nehemiah was firm in his choice.

Sadly, many believers are not wise when the enemies call in sweet, soothing voices to make peace with them by compromising the work of God. Oh, it doesn't seem so bad at first; it probably seems very harmless and in fact may be logical to attempt peace. But that is also the last thought of a bird that gets trapped in a snare and killed! It is not harmless and not logical for there is NO way to reconcile good and evil. If there is a compromise made between them, truth is lost! Anything less than truth is a lie! Evil ALWAYS wins when truth is compromised or when morals are set aside for certain situations. Evil's only desire and design is to do harm in a believer's life. No good ever can or will come from being at peace with evil.

Beware, believer, evil tries to appear innocent and good. It is very persuasive and persistent, but it must not be heeded. Avoid it by knowing it. Know it by knowing God. Know God by studying and heeding to His Word. Remember, no matter what we think, evil will always be evil. Evil will never be anything but evil, and it always leads to destruction. Turn to Christ, trust in Christ; and triumph in Christ over evil!!!!

> *Then sent Sanballat his servant unto me in like manner the fifth time with an open letter in his hand; Wherein was written, It is reported among the heathen, and Gashmu saith it, that thou and the Jews think to rebel: for which cause thou buildest the wall, that thou mayest be their king, according to these words. And thou hast also appointed prophets to preach of Thee at Jerusalem, saying, There is a king in Judah: and now shall it be reported to the king according to these words. Come now therefore, and let us take counsel together. Then I sent unto him, saying, There are no such things done as thou sayest, but thou feignest them out of thine own heart. For they all made us afraid, saying, Their hands shall be weakened from the work, that it be not done. Now therefore, O God, strengthen my hands.*
> - Nehemiah 6:5-9

The enemy was infuriated that their plans had failed thus far. Frustrated and infuriated, the enemy resorted to more fierce means in an effort to prevent the building of the wall. Sanballat sent Nehemiah an open letter in which was written a very false, dangerous report about them. If this lie reached the Persian King, it meant death for the Persians did not have time or mercy for even the slightest hint of rebellion. Sanballat's report not only claimed Nehemiah wanted to be king, but that he had even hired prophets to "foretell" of his rule! Then Sanballat "kindly" ended by offering to meet with Nehemiah and clear this whole thing up. One can almost see him smugly smirking to himself as he writes this!

This whole thing, however, is nothing more than an ancient form of gossip and blackmail. An open letter is like a megaphone: it's for whoever happens to be around the area to hear. It's gossip, which is truly dangerous and destructive. The "kind" invitation was only blackmail. Believers should never be surprised by the world's attempts to ruin our testimonies and prevent our work for God. Even Christ was lied about, slandered, and mocked.

Nehemiah didn't let this upset him though. He simply stated the truth to combat the lie. He knew where the source was. He also knew why: to cause fear to stop the work. So he prayed that God would enable him to work all the harder.

A believer should never let gossip cause him to stop working for God. He should speak the truth and not get carried away defending himself instead of working. He should pray, live right, and work all the harder that his actions combat the lies and the work gets done!!!!

Afterward I came unto the house of Shemaiah the son of Delaiah the son of Mehetabeel, who was shut up; and he said, Let us meet together in the house of God, within the temple, and let us shut the doors of the temple: for they will come to slay thee; yea, in the night will they come to slay thee. And I said, Should such a man as I flee? and who is there, that, being as I am, would go into the temple to save his life? I will not go in. And, lo, I perceived that God had not sent him; but that he pronounced this prophecy against me: for Tobiah and Sanballat had hired him. Therefore was he hired, that I should be afraid, and do so, and sin, and that they might have matter for an evil report, that they might reproach me. My God, think Thou upon Tobiah and Sanballat according to these their works, and on the prophetess Noadiah, and the rest of the prophets, that would have put me in fear.
- Nehemiah 6:10-14

This attempt of Sanballat and Tobiah was neither a threat or blackmail, but was trickery. As in all their attempts, it too was to cause discouragement and fear, and ultimately stop them from building the wall. Shemaiah told him of a plot to slay him - which was indeed true and probably not surprising to Nehemiah. This plot, however, was different: it was to get him to flee into the temple. With the wall nearing completion, Nehemiah knew the enemies were desperate to be rid of him, but how did he know that Shemaiah was hired to kill him?

He knew because Shemaiah told him to go into the temple which would be direct disobedience to God's law and an act punishable by death! So he knew God did not send him, and prayed that God would judge his enemies.

Sadly, many are not like Nehemiah. Paul warned and rebuked believers who were heeding "another gospel" which added works to repentance of sin and belief in Christ's death, burial, and resurrection. Paul said even if an angel preached differently than what God has already said, don't believe him! God does not, and cannot, change. The power of God to reconcile sinners to Himself is still through Christ alone. Repent of sin and believe in Christ; other ways are only death!!!!

So the wall was finished in the twenty and fifth day of the month Elul, in fifty and two days. And it came to pass, that when all our enemies heard thereof, and all the heathen that were about us saw these things, they were much cast down in their own eyes: for they perceived that this work was wrought of our God. - Nehemiah 6:15-16

Against all and at last, the wall of Jerusalem was completed. Had this been a project of mere man - even the most resolved man - it would not have been done. This, however, was no doing of man's abilities but of God's power. And when God's omnipotence is strengthening the work, not even all power of Hell can prevent its completion! Furthermore, just as the enemies of Nehemiah were forced to acknowledge, none will be able to deny that the work was begun, continued, and finished by the power of God alone. The entire world will bow before God and admit that He alone is God; even the powers of Hell will be forced to submit.

God would centuries later and against all complete an even greater work. This work was the greatest of all; it was the redemption of man. Man rebelled against God and faced eternity in Hell separated from God because of sin. There was NOTHING man could do to change this; even the best of men was still a sinner by nature and choice. There was a wall between God and man forever separating them unless God intervened. Thankfully, He did. His love sent His only Son, Christ, to Earth. Christ lived a perfect life from birth to death. Although He came only to save man, many rejected Him, and even his own apostles forsook Him in the end of His life. Christ was unmercifully beaten, mocked, and sentenced to death on the cross though He had done nothing wrong. On the cross, He bore ALL sin and its punishment, and died. He took our death. Then three days later, He rose from the dead. This finished the redemption of man's soul from sin; it broke down the wall between God and man. NOTHING could stop Him. Praise God!!!!

Moreover in those days the nobles of Judah sent many letters unto Tobiah, and the letters of Tobiah came unto them. For there were many in Judah sworn unto him, because he was the son in law of Shechaniah the son of Arah; and his son Johanan had taken the daughter of Meshullam the son of Berechiah. Also they reported his good deeds before me, and uttered my words to him. And Tobiah sent letters to put me in fear.

- Nehemiah 6:17-19

Here is where we find how the enemies stayed so well informed and just how deep Nehemiah's problems were in Jerusalem. It wasn't a spy secretly sneaking around, nor was it a turncoat informing the enemies; it was the Jewish nobles openly and devoutly helping Tobiah! One would think they would recognize him as an enemy - especially since he slandered them. They, however, didn't! They were sworn to him by a marriage and probably financially as well. Moreover, it wasn't just lawful loyalty, but loving loyalty! They thought he was good and not just thought it, but tried to convince Nehemiah of it! They surely believed Tobiah over Nehemiah and saw Nehemiah as bad! "But how?" we may ask. "How could they be so blind?" They were willingly blind, the worst blind of all. They saw and believed only what they wanted, only what was convenient for them. Their lust for wealth and power blinded them to the evil of Tobiah; it blinded them so well they called evil good and good evil.

We may think that this could never happen to us, it's too ridiculous, and we're smarter than that. Sadly, we are not. When our focus moves from Christ to the world, we begin to love the world. The longer we stay that way the stronger the lust becomes; we grow blinder by the second. Then when confronted about our sin, we excuse it and call it "good for us". See how quickly we can change to call evil good! It may be a matter of convenience (it's this or worst) but evil can ALWAYS be avoided. It may be a matter of cash (it's this or not pay bills, etc.) but if you do as God wills, He will take care of everything. In everything, acting against God - even in the littlest matter - leads to destruction. Acting as God wills isn't easy, but is best in all things. It is easy to be blinded but difficult to acknowledge and accept when revealed. BE CAREFUL; keep you eyes on Christ and don't be blinded by the world!!!!

> *Now it came to pass, when the wall was built, and I had set up the doors, and the porters and the singers and the Levites were appointed, that I gave my brother Hanani, and Hananiah the ruler of the palace, charge over Jerusalem: for he was a faithful man, and feared God above many. And I said unto them, Let not the gates of Jerusalem be opened until the sun be hot; and while they stand by, let them shut the doors, and bar them: and appoint watches of the inhabitants of Jerusalem, every one in his watch, and every one to be over against his house.* - Nehemiah 7:1-3

The walls were built, but that did not eliminate the enemies. They still hated Nehemiah and the wall, and they were still being informed by the nobles of Jerusalem about all that was happening within the wall!

This, however, did not deter Nehemiah's appointing of singers and Levites to lead the people in worship to God. God had protected and provided for them and enabled them to build the wall despite much persecution. This was a victory for them, and they owed it to God. Therefore, they worshiped Him. God has ultimately given victory to all who repent of their sins and believe in Christ. This eternal victory is over sin in our daily lives; we can live for Him. Finally, He will give us ultimate victory when He returns and gives us glorified bodies; sin will be no more! For each of these glorious victories He gives us, we must worship Him and thank Him. That is the first thing we must do. It acknowledges to all that we are not victorious on our own, but only by God through Christ.

Then, we must not disregard the fact that the enemy is still out there. Thinking we are safe without further effort is vain and a big head only makes for an easier target! Thus, we must continue to watch and have trusted others who help us stay doing right. Just as Nehemiah appointed men to watch the walls, we must watch and accept watch. A battle may be won, but the war isn't over 'til Christ returns and banishes sin forever. A wall may be built, but it won't watch for itself! Therefore, let us watch continually and worship constantly!!!!

Now the city was large and great: but the people were few therein, and the houses were not builded. And my God put into mine heart to gather together the nobles, and the rulers, and the people, that they might be reckoned by genealogy. And I found a register of the genealogy of them which came up at the first, and found written therein, These are the children of the province, that went up out of the captivity, of those that had been carried away, whom Nebuchadnezzar the king of Babylon had carried away, and came again to Jerusalem and to Judah, every one unto his city; Who came with Zerubbabel, Jeshua, Nehemiah, Azariah, Raamiah, Nahamani, Mordecai, Bilshan, Mispereth, Bigvai, Nehum, Baanah. The number, I say, of the men of the people of Israel was this; - Nehemiah 7:4-7

Having completed the wall, Nehemiah didn't sit back and take a break. He put his brother and the one who first told him about the sad state of Jerusalem in charge of the city wall and its guards. Nehemiah now turned his attention to another problem: the people were few, and the houses were not built. How could Jerusalem prosper in their new walled city if there weren't many people living in it, and many who did live in it were poor?

God once again laid a mission on Nehemiah's heart. He wasn't finished with Nehemiah in Jerusalem yet. Let us remember that as long as we are here, God has a purpose for us too. One finished job doesn't mean we're finished. We may not have a "big picture" immediately after we complete one, but it is in those times of waiting that we fine tune our brushes, paints, and skills. It is during the times of waiting for God to reveal to us our next "big step of faith" that we prepare by doing the things we know God wants all of His children to do.

Nehemiah's new task was to correctly number and place each returnee in their tribe. One's tribe in Israel's beginning determined not only where he lived, but what he could and couldn't do. It was vital to each Israelite, but many of these had lost it in captivity. Nehemiah was to organize and purify the people - a great task indeed! God, however, had already supplied what was needed; a scroll with all the names of the returnees (read verses 8-60, 66-69). God always provides one with the tools needed to get His will done!!!!

And these were they which went up also from Telmelah, Telharesha, Cherub, Addon, and Immer: but they could not shew their father's house, nor their seed, whether they were of Israel. The children of Delaiah, the children of Tobiah, the children of Nekoda, six hundred forty and two. And of the priests: the children of Habaiah, the children of Koz, the children of Barzillai, which took one of the daughters of Barzillai the Gileadite to wife, and was called after their name. These sought their register among those that were reckoned by genealogy, but it was not found: therefore were they, as polluted, put from the priesthood. And the Tirshatha said unto them, that they should not eat of the most holy things, till there stood up a priest with Urim and Thummim. - Nehemiah 7:61-65

Among those seeking to prove their genealogy was a family claiming to be priest. However, they could not prove who they said they were. Thus they were considered as those who polluted the priesthood and were put out of all priestly services until a priest could determine God's will by the Urim and Thummin, a thing which God used to tell them His will.

Nehemiah never said these people were bad or even that they weren't priest; he just said they couldn't prove it and thus had to be disqualified until God directed otherwise. This may seem very unfair, but let us consider the consequences of allowing them to continue just because they wanted to do so. 1) The priesthood, those mediators between God and Israel, would have been polluted. If the middle link is bad, then the chain is weak and not as strong as it could be. The result would be disastrous for both priest and people. God set the rules for His worship and accepts nothing less; there is no blessing for those who go against Him. 2) It could have led to their death. God didn't judge lightly those who polluted the priesthood. At one time, thousands died! Uzziah's only downfall as king was polluting the priesthood, but God struck him with leprosy; he was cast from the city, died, and was remembered only as a leper!

The priesthood was an honorable role, but dangerous to envy.

God has a place and purpose for each person. One should desire only to be where God wills him to be. It is only there that God will receive the most honor and glory from his life!!!!

And some of the chief of the fathers gave unto the work. The Tirshatha gave to the treasure a thousand drams of gold, fifty basons, five hundred and thirty priests' garments. And some of the chief of the fathers gave to the treasure of the work twenty thousand drams of gold, and two thousand and two hundred pound of silver. And that which the rest of the people gave was twenty thousand drams of gold, and two thousand pound of silver, and threescore and seven priests' garments. So the priests, and the Levites, and the porters, and the singers, and some of the people, and the Nethinims, and all Israel, dwelt in their cities; and when the seventh month came, the children of Israel were in their cities. - Nehemiah 7:70-73

After having built the wall and been counted, the first act recorded of the people was their willful giving to the house of God! What a marvelous thing to have done first. There's nothing better that could have been done than giving to God for all He has given to them. They were preparing the temple and priest for the worship of God and in doing thus preparing themselves to worship God. How? God commanded Israel to take care of the priest so that the priest may in turn take care of them and the temple. By giving to the temple and priest, the people were obeying God. The first act of worship preparation is obedience to God, for how can one worship God when he is against God in his heart?! Then the heart of the giver will be blessed and his gift will be well-pleasing to God. If a heart is not right with God, the offering is nothing to God. He desires obedience from a humble heart more than He desires sacrifices.

After God has blessed us, what is our first act of response? Do we give it back to Him by using it for His honor and glory, or do we squander it on self and waste it? Sadly, many times we waste it. In truth, every breath is a blessing from God. Thus every breath should be given back in obedience to God; if it's not, it's wasted. We may not have much money to give to God (and what we have we should give), but we do have our lives. By giving ourselves in obedience to God, we're ready to worship God by giving of our possessions and life to His honor and glory!!!!

And all the people gathered themselves together as one man into the street that was before the water gate; and they spake unto Ezra the scribe to bring the book of the law of Moses, which the LORD had commanded to Israel. And Ezra the priest brought the law before the congregation both of men and women, and all that could hear with understanding, upon the first day of the seventh month. - Nehemiah 8:1-2

The people prepared for the worship of God: the priests, singers, and porters had been set; their hearts were prepared by their obedience to God; and they readied the tabernacle and priests by their gifts. Obedience and sacrifice were requirements for each individual who desired to worship God. Now they gathered together as one man in spirit and in truth.

For God's people to worship Him they must come in unity; God is a God of order. If His people are in discord, there is no way for them to worship God. They must be one in spirit. God is Spirit and those desiring to worship Him must do so in spirit. Because of our sin nature, however, our spirits are dead unto God. In the flesh, we can't worship God for all our goodness from our flesh is as filthy, stinky rags before Him. Repentance of sin and faith in Christ's perfect death and resurrection for us is the ONLY way for our spirits to be made alive unto God and able to worship Him. Only those alive to God can come in unity of spirit to worship Him.

Then Israel had unity in their desire for truth. God is truth and can't look favorably on any form of sin; all sin is lies. Thus those desiring to worship God must be in the unity of the truth of His Word. Israel asked for God's Word. They didn't want self-help/esteem books or any words of men, but only the perfect Word of God. Only upon it can man build his life and know for sure that he is right and safe with God!!!!

And he read therein before the street that was before the water gate from the morning until midday, before the men and the women, and those that could understand; and the ears of all the people were attentive unto the book of the law. And Ezra the scribe stood upon a pulpit of wood, which they had made for the purpose; and beside him stood Mattithiah, and Shema, and Anaiah, and Urijah, and Hilkiah, and Maaseiah, on his right hand; and on his left hand, Pedaiah, and Mishael, and Malchiah, and Hashum, and Hashbadana, Zechariah, and Meshullam. - Nehemiah 8:3-4

    Israel had gathered in unity of desire to hear God's Word. Now Ezra stood on a pulpit and read to them, to all of them who could understand. He did this from morning to evening, and the people listened attentively. They had such a strong desire for God's Word that they listened attentively to it for hours, hours that could have been spent on other things.

    For God's people to worship Him, they not only must come in unity of spirit and truth, but also listen attentively to God's Word. What good does it do to come to hear God's Word if we do not listen to it?! Why should we come to worship God if we are going to be double-minded about it? We have a bad habit of double-mindedness, also known as "letting one's mind wander" or "daydreaming". Our focus isn't on God's Word, but on the world. We cannot listen attentively to God and be wandering aimlessly in our thoughts. It's not possible. Therefore, we must train and discipline - for it does take practice and perseverance - ourselves to come before God single-mindedly, focused, and set on listening to God, no distractions dangling like baited hooks in the back of our minds.

    The people also came willing to spend time listening to God. This was much longer than a 30-45 minute message; it was hours! Are we that dedicated to God that we would sacrifice to Him hours of our day? We should be. Nothing is more important!!!!

And Ezra opened the book in the sight of all the people; (for he was above all the people;) and when he opened it, all the people stood up:
- Nehemiah 8:5

Along with unity and attentiveness/desire, God's people must have respect toward God and His Word in order to worship Him. God doesn't just accept whatever we drag into church and dump onto the pew. As our Creator and Sustainer He desires, deserves, and demands our absolute and utmost respect. That is how it should be. If there is no respect, there is no reverence; without reverence, there is no worship. Think! Worship is the act of reverence and respect! So one can come to worship, but not worship at all for it is more than just showing up, singing, and studying. It is respect shown by our attire, actions, and attentiveness. All of that should be nothing but our best. We should look our best and act our best; it should bring God honor and glory. It is not about our convenience and comfort (there has been, is, and will be for us a time when that has NOTHING to do with God's worship for God's worshipers will be persecuted!) but all about reverence and glory to God.

When Ezra opened God's Word, the people stood in honor of God's Word. Today, many people stand in honor of many things - our military, judges, etc -, and while that is not a bad thing, how many of those same people have dust on their Bibles or have a Bible!? God's Word isn't just another book; it is the holy, complete, eternal words of God. All that it says is true and right, whether or not man agrees with it. Man is not the judge of the Bible. If he attepmts that, God, the Author, will judge him; and what man can say God is wrong. God and God alone is the only standard of right and wrong! The Bible judges man. We're privileged to have it. Respect it; care for it; obey it!!!!

And Ezra blessed the LORD, the great God. And all the people answered, Amen, Amen, with lifting up their hands: and they bowed their heads, and worshipped the LORD with their faces to the ground.
                                                    - Nehemiah 8:6

    The people came together in unity; they had a desire for the truth of God's Word; they had attentiveness to it; and they had respect for it. Now, we see they had humility. Without humility, worship isn't God approved: He rejects pride. Sadly, this type of false worship is very common. People meet in unity with a desire to hear God's Word; they even pay close attention - maybe even be able to quote it flawlessly - and hold it in great respect during worship. They do all this, however, for the gratification of their flesh; it makes them feel good. Thus it was with the most respected religious sect of Jesus' day, the Pharisees. In the eyes of men, they were holy. In the eyes of God, they were hypocrites. Yes, it's very true, scary, and deadly: the flesh can masquerade itself into and under the worship of God. God without fail knows though and will judge it.

    What is so appealing about the Pharisees was that they were doing what the law required in the strictest sense! The way of the flesh doesn't have to be drugs, adulatory, fornication, murder, lies, hate, and etc.... That is how many believe it to be; and yes it is, but it is not only that. It can be the direct opposite! That is where many desiring to be righteous actually fall to their fleshly desires. That is where we find people like the Pharisee. These people are unyieldingly strict in the observances of the law. This is also where we find the people of Colossians 2:18-23. The Syncretism practiced and taught that matter was evil and only a harsh rejection of the body would lead to holiness. And in this company we find also the flagellants who beat themselves with whips as punishment for their sins. No one does these things anymore! Yes, these sects are still active, just renamed: "Salvation by works", Hinduism, Buddhism, etc.... The problem with these is that they appeal to the flesh's drive by appalling the flesh's desires - like focusing on the symptoms and not the sickness. It makes one seem and believe he is well when he is not! These give men a false sense of righteousness, one that is due to their works. This in turn makes men proud; and that leads to rejection of God. Beware! Focus on what God has done for you; it's more than all you can do for Him. Be humble and worship Him!!!!

Also Jeshua, and Bani, and Sherebiah, Jamin, Akkub, Shabbethai, Hodijah, Maaseiah, Kelita, Azariah, Jozabad, Hanan, Pelaiah, and the Levites, caused the people to understand the law: and the people stood in their place. So they read in the book in the law of God distinctly, and gave the sense, and caused them to understand the reading. - Nehemiah 8:7-8

Is there any point at all for anyone to read this if the only one who could understand it is me? NO! It would be a complete waste of everyone's time: my time for writing what no one could understand, and your time for reading the babble. There would be no purpose. The same point applies to worship. A most important part of worship is the reading of God's Word, but to what does it profit anyone if it is not understood? If one leaves the worship of God remembering only how eloquently the preacher spoke, or baffled by the mass amounts of unexplained knowledge poured into his mind, or only able to quote the funny or sad stories, or even with the desire to better himself but not because of a better understanding of God's Word, then the time spent reading or listening to God's Word is not profitable. The speaker wasted his breath and the hearer his ears.

Paul warned of this in 1 Corinthians 1:17-2:5. If any man could have boasted in his knowledge, spoken intelligently over people's level of understanding, or caused people to follow him, it was Paul. He could quote the first five books of the Bible; he argued intelligently against the masters of philosophy of his world - and persuaded some! He even had believers in Corinth saying they were of Paul - which he did correct their pride in him. And God sent him to the Gentiles, the non-Jews, those who were considered foolish, dumb, and vile.

A greater - and the best - example of a teacher of God is Christ Himself! Robed in flesh was the omniscience - all knowing - God. Yet He did not speak with great swelling words to awe and baffle people, and did not tell needless stories to entertain them. He spoke so that everyone could understand should they truly desire to do so. The unfathomable knowledge of God was explained in the common words of every day man. This was so man could understand and glorify God, not the speaker.

When we worship God, let us seek to understand His Word that our lives may truly be able to change by it. And should we be sharing God's Word, let us do so not to impress or entertain but to cause one to understand more of God's Word and glorify Him!!!!

And Nehemiah, which is the Tirshatha, and Ezra the priest the scribe, and the Levites that taught the people, said unto all the people, This day is holy unto the LORD your God; mourn not, nor weep. For all the people wept, when they heard the words of the law. - Nehemiah 8:9

The people showed their respect and humility before God for who He is. Now, they showed humility to God for who they were. When we show humility before God because of who He is, we are acting upon our knowledge of Him: God alone, sovereign, eternal, holy. When we show humility before God for who we are, we act upon our knowledge of how God sees us: sinners, rebellious, hell-bound and deserving. It's the difference between knowing someone and knowing how that someone sees you. You won't know how someone else sees you unless they tell you, all else is speculation.

This is what happened to Israel and what should happen to us when we worship God. Our hearts should be broken over sin. Sadly, and much to OUR detriment, this necessity of worship is under constant discredit, abuse, and disgust. People don't want to feel badly about their lives and sin; they want to feel good about themselves and not find out - much less focus on - the fact that all are sinners self-doomed to hell without Christ. Thus, this humility is deemed belittling, politically incorrect, and bashing. In many places it is thrown out, ignored, or lost. This, however, is more deadly than if people weren't told they had a terminal but curable illness! The wages of sin is eternal death, but the gift of God through Christ is eternal life. We desperately need to be crushed in our hearts about sin.

Israel wept over the sin the Word of God revealed in their lives. This was a GOOD thing because it led to repentance of sin and forgiveness in Christ. Jesus said, "Blessed are they that mourn; for they will be comforted." David says, "A broken and contrite heart Thou wilt not despise", "Blessed is he whose iniquities are forgiven." And that is where weeping turns to rejoicing, at forgiveness. But this is also where many reject this humility because their weeping doesn't lead to repentance. They want sin AND the blessings of forgiveness, but it can't be done. Humble yourself, repent, and rejoice in forgiveness!!!!

Then he said unto them, Go your way, eat the fat, and drink the sweet, and send portions unto them for whom nothing is prepared: for this day is holy unto our LORD: neither be ye sorry; for the joy of the LORD is your strength. So the Levites stilled all the people, saying, Hold your peace, for the day is holy; neither be ye grieved. - Nehemiah 8:10-11

☺!!!

The people came before God with hearts broken over sin. They repented of their sin, turned from sin and to God. They wanted a good relationship with God, and because they repented and believed, God restored their relationship with Him.

Ezra told the people because they repented, God had forgiven them. He does the same for anyone. If anyone confesses his sins - confess meaning to see sin as God sees it - God is faithful and just to forgive him of his sins and to cleanse him from all unrighteousness. And God can do so too because Christ died to afford us all forgiveness. There isn't a single sin for which Christ didn't die, so there isn't one sin God can't forgive completely if one repents.

Then Ezra told them to celebrate, because the joy of the LORD was their strength. The time for mourning was over; the time of rejoicing had come. Ezra did not say go and do good because you need to pay God back for forgiving you, nor did he say to go do good to relieve your guilt. All that had been done and done away with. Forgiveness was completely bought by Christ's death, and guilt was banished by forgiveness.

Many have great difficulty with guilt. After they are forgiven, they needlessly bear it. They do this because they can't believe they are forgiven or so that it will motivate them to do the right thing. Both of these, however, are wrong. Guilt is good and has its purpose, but that purpose doesn't reach beyond the outstretched arms of forgiveness. Guilt bore after forgiveness may drive us to do good for a while, but it won't last that way; it will eventually harden our hearts to the conviction of God and make us very bitter. That is why the joy of the Lord that we have in forgiveness - NOT guilt - is our strength, our motivator. Be forgiven; release guilt and embrace joy!!!!

And all the people went their way to eat, and to drink, and to send portions, and to make great mirth, because they had understood the words that were declared unto them.   - Nehemiah 8:12

    The people broke their hearts over sin and mourned before God. Then God forgave them, and the priest told them to rejoice. God wanted them to rejoice in His forgiving of their sins; there was no more reason to have guilt or be sorry because God forgave them of it. Now they needed to rejoice; now they needed to do God's will with joy in their hearts - not guilt - but love for God who forgave them. The people submitted to God's Word by their rejoicing and sharing.

    Worship doesn't end at humility or even rejoicing. True worship doesn't end; it continues into everyday life by submission and obedience to God's Word. This is vital to worship, the proper and right affect of all other parts of worship: unity, desire for truth, attentiveness, respect, humility, and rejoicing. Obedience is the test of true worship. NOTE OF IMPORTANCE: True worship doesn't and can't have an either-or heart in any of its parts. Every part of worship depends and is an application to every other part of worship. Obedience without the other parts of worship is nothing but hypocrisy. David said in Psalm 51, "You do not desire sacrifice... the sacrifices of God are a broken spirit." The book of Malachi is all about the disgust of God toward those who "obey" but without humility. Jesus Himself called them "white washed sepulchers full of dead man's bones." On the other side, one can't truly have the other parts of worship and not obey! One can't claim to love the Lord and not obey Him; again it's hypocrisy. The book of James reprimands these types of people. Jesus said a tree is known by its fruit and a man by his deeds whether they be good or evil. They talk the talk but don't walk to match it. They worship on Sunday but live for self on the other days.

    Worship is a privilege; the abuse of it is a terrible problem and shame of today. Love the Lord thy God with all your heart, soul, and mind; fear God and keep his commandments. Worship God!!!!

And on the second day were gathered together the chief of the fathers of all the people, the priests, and the Levites, unto Ezra the scribe, even to understand the words of the law.   - Nehemiah 8:13

After Israel's revival, those who explained scriptures were tired but excited. So, on the second day, they did not return immediately out to the people but rather retreated unto themselves and gathered to Ezra. It is not selfish, lazy, or uncaring for teachers to rest. There is no shame in being completely exhausted after a long day of work. The shame would be in being tired without good reason. Proverbs states that the lazy are like creaking doors; a lazy man will turn from side to side, accomplish nothing, and still be tired. God made man and told him to work, but God also made man a day of rest. Jesus, Himself, withdrew from teaching and rested for hours; He told His disciples to do the same. It is good to rest for in that time you can be renewed as you review all the wonderful things God has done and draw closer to God.

    Here we find the teachers retreating but not simply to rest; they went to be taught. No one knows everything - especially those who think they do. Wise men know that there is no end to learning. The more one learns the more one knows that he doesn't know it all. Thus it is good to be taught. Another teacher may have more insight into certain scriptures. There is no new revelation of scripture, but there is abundant illumination of it. And since no one man can ever know all there is to know about the Bible, all men need to continually study and be taught about it. The Bible can reveal something new to you at every study!!!!

And they found written in the law which the LORD had commanded by Moses, that the children of Israel should dwell in booths in the feast of the seventh month: And that they should publish and proclaim in all their cities, and in Jerusalem, saying, Go forth unto the mount, and fetch olive branches, and pine branches, and myrtle branches, and palm branches, and branches of thick trees, to make booths, as it is written.
- Nehemiah 8:14-15

All of Israel's feast days were for the purpose of remembering what God had done for them. God made this day to remind them of His love and care for them when they wandered in the wilderness forty years because of their lack of faith in Him and thus disobedience to Him. They were not to forget lest they should repeat the sin.

Forgetting, however, was exactly what they did. The darkness of their sin steadily blackened their hearts and minds until their feast days were lost, and for centuries of sin and more sin they forgot what God had done for them and did that which was right in their own eyes. Forgetfulness causes repetition. That is why remembering what God has done and what He requires is vital to our worship and obedience.

Now, the teachers sought to understand God's Word, and God revealed to them His will. God and His will never changes. It was the same for them as it was their forefathers who allowed it to be forgotten. God wanted them to remember. It had not changed just as their past had not changed. It fell into obscurity but was still there in the Law. Just because God's laws and will may be unpopular - for that is how forgetfulness begins - or forgotten, it doesn't mean they have changed or aren't there anymore. It means man must repent!

How easy it is to forget God's will; we tend to excuse our actions rather than repent. Forgetfulness happens dangerously quick, but its consequences can pass down through generations. Remember God's doings; seek His will; trust Him and keep His Word!!!!

So the people went forth, and brought them, and made themselves booths, every one upon the roof of his house, and in their courts, and in the courts of the house of God, and in the street of the water gate, and in the street of the gate of Ephraim. And all the congregation of them that were come again out of the captivity made booths, and sat under the booths: for since the days of Jeshua the son of Nun unto that day had not the children of Israel done so. And there was very great gladness. - Nehemiah 8:16-17

Having heard the Word of their God, the people immediately set to work to do it. They did not drag their feet or run their mouths with questions or excuses. They heard and went forth. It didn't matter that they had just finished a full day revival and were probably tired. It didn't matter that this feast day had not been observed by them for centuries. The only thing that did matter to them was that God had told them to do it and now was the time.

How wonderful it would be if all people had such a submissive spirit at all times toward God's Word! This is not the case sadly. Many make excuses not to do God's Word immediately. Before he turns to God and from sin, before he believes in Christ's death and resurrection for us, he wants to "sow his wild oats" without a care that his own sinful soul is as a tare ready to be cast at any breath into Hell's eternal flames to burn. We hoard our lives and lose them anyway. Even those who know Christ as their Savior and can live for God drag their feet, at times. They sometimes stumble and fall, excusing themselves so that they can dabble happily - but happy won't last - in the filthy, stinky mire of sin. How pitiful and pathetic we are when we do such. And this leads only to shame.

Note then the outcome of obeying God immediately -- Great Gladness. Blissful Contentment. May we always hear and heed God immediately that He may bless us with great gladness!!!!

Now in the twenty and fourth day of this month, the children of Israel were assembled with fasting, and with sackclothes, and earth upon them. And the seed of Israel separated themselves from all strangers, and stood and confessed their sins, and the iniquities of their fathers. – Nehemiah 9:1-2

Not long after they kept the feast, many of Israel joined in a fast of repentance. But weren't they just repenting right before the feast?! Yes, they were. Repentance, however, is not a one-time thing but an as-many-times-as-you-need-it thing. There is no number to how many times one can repent. We all sin every day; it would be good for us, therefore, to repent every day.

The people repented with fasting, sack-clothes and earth. They went without food, dressed in a burlap-sack type outfit and put dirt on their heads. This to us may sound extreme, but they were showing their humility to God and man. They wanted to show that nothing was more important – not food, comfort, pride, friends or family – as repentance, as being forgiven by God and brought back into fellowship with Him. They "separated themselves from all strangers" those who would encourage and draw them away from God and to false gods. Then they stood before everyone else and confessed that they were sinners who came from sinners – generations of rebellion against God; they were guilty by nature and choices. Therefore, nothing was more important to them as rejecting sin and turning to God for forgiveness and fellowship with Him.

How important is forgiveness and fellowship with God to us? Does our sinful nature and actions make us sick, make us feel disgusted, humble us before our holy Creator and Sustainer? We tend to have a casual and even cordial, at times, attitude toward sin! We think our sin nature is an excuse for our sin actions, but it is not. We don't let sin bother us because we know we'll sin every day anyway. We take for granite God's forgiveness and fellowship because Christ paid for it with His blood and it's always there for us when we repent. So we enjoy sin because we know we can be forgiven. "God understands". If God "understood", He wouldn't command us to be holy! Forgiveness and fellowship are precious, priceless privileges. Treasure them and sin not!!!!

And they stood up in their place, and read in the book of the Law of their LORD their God one fourth part of the day; and another fourth part they confessed their sins and worshipped the LORD their God.
— Nehemiah 9:3

After their humble repentance, Israel read God's Word, acknowledged who they were and worshipped God. This should be the response of every repentant heart. Repentance is not for the purpose nor is its desired effect in any way for us to just feel good about ourselves again. The Pharisees abused it – by merely acting repentant but not being so – for such a reason they weren't even forgiven! If its only end was to make us feel good, we have no need of it because obviously we can feel good even in sin. Therefore, the purpose of repentance is that we may be forgiven by God; and while forgiveness does make us feel better, that is not its end either!

Forgiveness isn't only for making us feel better. True, it removes our guiltiness before God and thus our guilt, but its purpose is much deeper and richer than that – and thank God that it is! Forgiveness is for the purpose of bringing us into fellowship with God. This makes it possible for God to abundantly bless us with all that is good. This, however and still, is not the only reason for forgiveness. Yes, thankfully, it is more magnificently glorious than that! We don't receive forgiveness and blessing to hoard them or waste them on ourselves – though sadly many do so. The purpose of forgiveness is that we may bring honor and glory to God. There's no greater purpose for anything than that purpose for which it is made: to honor God. There's no beyond that, and short of it is vain. Forgiveness is to draw us closer to God that we by obedience may worship Him to His honor and glory. It's about God!!!!

SMILE!!! SCRIPTURE STUDIES: Nehemiah

And they stood up upon the stairs, of the Levites, Jeshua, and Bani, Kadmiel, Shebaniah, Bunni, Sherebiah, Bani, and Chanani, and cried with a loud voice unto the LORD of their God. Then the Levites, Jeshua, and Kadmiel, Bani, Hashabniah, Sherebiah, Hodijah, Shebaniah, and Pethahiah, said, Stand up and bless the LORD your God for ever and ever; and blessed be Thy glorious name, which is exalted above all blessing and praise. – Nehemiah 9:4-5

What does it mean to be exalted above all blessing and praise? It means there is no praise and blessing that one can give that could accurately capture and portray just how magnificent and worthy God is. How truly unfathomable our God is! All of heaven and earth will one day bow before Him and join in an eternal, thunderous chorus of adoration and worship of God and not even then shall there be found an end! As you read, right now, the heavens are declaring the glory of God in every language, to every person, throughout the entire universe, and without end. How awesome our God is.

He is not just beyond praise because of who He is; He is so because of what He has done. He, knowing we would rebel and plummet all creation into sin, created us and loved us. He already knew and had a plan to save us from sin, eternal death in separation from God. He sent His Son to bear our sin and its punishment for us. There is no greater show of love than that. Furthermore, we only have to turn from sin and to God and believe in Christ. There's nothing more we need to do to accept God's provision, and it's a "forever kind of provision" – no matter what. The gift of God is ETERNAL LIFE! Truly, He is beyond all praise and blessing, so let us worship Him now and forever!!!!

Thou, even thou, art LORD alone; Thou hast made heaven, the heaven of heavens, with all their host, the earth, and all things that are therein, the seas, and all that is therein, and Thou preserves them all; and the host of heaven worshipeth Thee. – Nehemiah 9:6

Having exclaimed that God is greater than all praise no matter how glorious or long it last, the leader then begins to explain why God is so great. NOTE: God is great whether or not man acknowledges Him or not; acknowledgement doesn't make God great or greater; anything man states about God doesn't affect His greatness; not even His acts make Him great (for He was great to have done them): they are just how we know He is great; they are an effect not a cause of His greatness.

Now, we know God is great because of His creation. Creation is our first and natural revelation of God. We ourselves are creations of God, molded in His very image by His own hands. At the moment of conception, each tiny, frail being speaks volumes toward the magnificence of God. And at that moment, we are blessed with an inward knowledge of God's existence. Then at birth, we are able to view the wonders of God's world and know He made it. Man may try to deny it, but it is still there. The cries of praise to God cannot be suffocated out by any amount of denial. He made the heavens and earth and all therein; He sustains it all and all worship Him. Join the thunderous chorus and praise to God who alone is God, Creator and Sustainer of all things!!!!

> *Thou are the LORD the God, who didst choose Abram, and broughtest him forth out of Ur of the Chaldeas, and gavest him the name of Abraham; And foundest his heart faithful before Thee, and madest a covenant with him to give the land of the Canaanites, the Httites, the Amorites, and the Perizzites, and the Jebusites, and the Girgashites, to give it, I say, to his seed, and hast performed Thy words; and Thou are righteous.*
>
> - Nehemiah 9:7-8

When praying to and/or worshipping God, it is always a good thing to recall the wonderful things God has already done. Whether it happened to you or someone else, it is good to remember. The Israelites remembered their father Abraham and the covenant God made with him because he was faithful to God; he wasn't perfect, but he did believe God despite everything. At 100 years and 90 years of age, Abraham and Sarah finally had their first child, the child whom God promised decades earlier. This child would make Abraham a great nation (viz_Israel). Through this child God promised Abraham to give his children the Promised Land. God kept His Word; and though Israel was in captivity for 70 years, they were now back in the land which God had promised them. And this happened not by war, but by the willing hand of their captor! Only God could have accomplished this. He kept His word because He is faithful.

God is the same today, tomorrow and forever. He is faithful to His children. Even when they rebel, He remains true to His Word, cares for them, chastens them, and fulfills His promises. This shouldn't encourage us to sin thinking it won't matter because God will stay faithful to us anyway (God does punish His own); this should cause us to love Him more and long to praise Him. Let us remember who God is and what He has done and let that burst forth in thankful prayer and praise!!!!

And didst see the affliction of our fathers in Egypt, and heardest their cry by the Red Sea; and showedst signs and wonders upon Pharaoh, and on all his servants; and on all the people of his land; for Thou knewest that they dealt proudly against them. So didst Thou get Thee a name, as it is this day. - Nehemiah 9:9-10

Israel continued to remember what God had done for them. God had not only seen and heard them but did deliver them from their hard bondage in Egypt. And when they were led to the Red Sea and began to complain against the Lord, He didn't reject them but delivered them again. He punished Egypt for their cruelty to Israel and their rejection of Him. He made Himself a name in their midst, such a name that terror of it reached some 250 miles away and had even the most fortified city, Jericho, trembling at the mere mention of it! Israel was an infant nation; it was not Israel that struck fear into the mightiest nations; it was the God of Israel! The God who alone is God!

So, what did God do? God proved He was God alone to Egypt. Each time pharaoh refused to release Israel, God did a miracle; water to blood, plague of frogs, flies, lice, cattle disease, boils on man and beast, hail, locust, tangible darkness, and lastly DEATH of all first born not protected by the blood of the Passover Lamb. Then God utterly destroyed the army of Egypt, the most powerful army in the world, in a single blow. God made Himself a name among them, and He will have Himself a name in every individual's life. He sent His son to die for us that we by turning from sin and believing Him can call Him Father. How will you choose to know Him!!!!

And Thou didst divide the sea before them, so that they went through the midst of the sea on dry land; and their persecutors Thou threwest into the deeps, as a stone into the mighty waters. - Nehemiah 9:11

    This is one of the pivotal acts in Israel's history: the day God delivered them from the Egyptians and made them a nation. Mountains on either side of them, the flooded Red Sea before them, and the world's most powerful army shaking the ground as they came to recapture them: it seemed hopeless. They began to complain and cry against God who brought them out of Egypt by the 10 plagues - how quickly we forget the awesome power of God when we view instead our awful circumstances. God, however, showed mercy to them, and parted the Red Sea so they could walk through it on dry ground! The enemy thundered behind them; but when Egypt was in the midst of the sea, the land turned to mud and they were helpless as the waves closed in on them like a book being slammed closed by the mighty hand of God. No one of the greatest army lived beyond that instant; they all died. Israel was delivered by the mighty hand of God.

    WOW! What deliverance! And we who know Christ as our Savior have an even more dramatic and magnificent deliverance! Having rebelled against God, man found himself surrounded by death and the Devil with his mighty army eager to take his soul to Hell to burn forever. God, however, showed mercy and sent His son to save us. Christ, as our sinless sacrifice, bore all sins and God's judgment as He died in our place. The enemies of God had seemingly won. Just then - 3 days later - the tight grip of death's hands burst open unable to hold Christ any longer than it was to hold Him. Sin, death and Hell were defeated forever! And that victory is ours when we reject sin, turn to God and believe in Christ. What an awesome deliverance we have in Christ!!!!

Moreover Thou leddest them in the day by a cloudy pillar; and in the night by a pillar of fire, to give them light in the way wherein they should go. - Nehemiah 9:12

What great mercy Israel experienced from God daily! In their prayer, they recalled with thanksgiving how God led them every day and night that they journeyed to the Promised Land. The cloud came and guided them when they left Egypt. It also protected them by lighting their way through the Red Sea but darkening beyond movement the way of the Egyptian army. It furthermore shielded them from the hot desert sun. The pillar of fire guided them at night and warmed them from the desert nights. Should Israel ever doubt that God was there or that He cared for them, they needed only look at the pillar of cloud or fire over them, guiding and protecting them. Even when they rebelled, complained and wished to return to Egypt or even die, God continued with them. And as they wandered 40 years in the wilderness for their faithlessness and disobedience, God stayed with them. Here, Israel remembered and thanked God for His mercy in guiding, protecting and being there for them always.

We today can thank God for the same reasons. No, we do not have a pillar guiding us, reminding us daily of God's presence and provision, but we do have something more assuring. It is even more assuring than the bodily - or glorified - presence of Christ Himself! Yes, even more than that. What is it? We have the Word of God. The Word of God is indeed more assurance than Israel has ever had in its past. In its pages are the beautiful precious promises of God who cannot lie or change. "I will never leave you or forsake you" - Hebrews 13:5. "Cast all your care upon Him for He cares for you" - 1 Peter 5:7. "My God will supply all your needs" - Philippians 4:19. We also have His guidance, "Thy word is a lamp unto my feet and a light unto my path". And any time we want we can find those precious, sacred words of God who loves us and cares for us; and in them, we can have restful assurance and joy for praise and thanks!!!!

> *Thou camest down also upon the Mount Sinai, and spakest with them from heaven and gavest them right judgments, and true laws, good statutes and commandments: And madest known unto them Thy holy Sabbath, and commandedst them precepts, statutes and laws, by the hand of Moses Thy servant.* - Nehemiah 9:13-14

Not only was Israel thankful for God's physical guidance but also for His spiritual guidance. This was the greatest thing He did for them; this is what set them apart from all other nations and made them special. No other nation had the revelation of God Himself through His commandments; they were guided by the darkness of their hearts, and anything "good" they had or did served not to their benefit of justification but their condemnation for they thus knew right but refused to acknowledge the one who is right, God. The greatest, most vital thing God gave the infant nation was what is right, true, good and holy; His laws.

Many today do not see rules - especially God's sadly - as being benevolent but brutal. And those who do gladly follow the rules are mocked as "goodie two-shoes", "bigots" and "self-righteous". Because God's commands don't conform to the world's desires and life, they reject them and even vehemently fight them. Man, however, is not the measure or maker of right or there would be no right! Why? Everyone would have his own standard. What would be right for one wouldn't be for another. Who can condemn murder, theft, etc. if each man is his own standard of right and wrong! There must be a standard and that must come from outside of man. That standard is God. Thanks be to Him who didn't leave us to our sin guided hearts and foolish imaginations but gave us His merciful, good laws!!!!

And gavest them bread from heaven for their hunger, and broughtest forth water for them out of the rock for their thirst, and promisedst them that they should go in to possess the land which Thou hadest sworn to give them.   - Nehemiah 9:15

Only three days after God destroyed the Egyptian army in the Red Sea, Israel was complaining against God and wishing they had never left Egypt. They were hot and wanted water, so God in His mercy led them to bitter water and turned it sweet for them and then led them to an Elam. Shortly thereafter, Israel was complaining against God and this time wishing God had destroyed them instead of delivered them. They were hungry, so God being rich in mercy gave them sweet, honey wafer bread from heaven every day of their journey to their land - over 40 years! However, when thirst struck again, Israel's complaining began again. God, thus, abundantly plenteous in mercy once again miraculously satisfied them with water from a rock, enough water to satisfy thousands of people and their animals! At last they came to the Promised Land, but once again they rebelled against God; they refused to enter the land because they feared the people whom God had promised to remove. God still in unfathomable mercy didn't destroy them but punished them with 40 years of wandering in the wilderness 'till they had died and their children would take the Promised Land. It is no wonder why Israel thanked God for His merciful provisions and promise.

    We may tend to believe Israel was terrible toward God and even discuss how blind and stupid they were; but before we condemn them with total disgust, let us remember our own lives. God is unfathomably merciful to us too. Israel's sin was focusing on their surroundings and not their Sustainer; this is faithlessness, rebellion. How many times a day do we find ourselves focused on our problems and not our Provider? Thank God for His mercy to us who are of little faith, and let us focus on God!!!!

But they and our fathers dealt proudly, and hardened their necks and hearkened not to Thy commandments, And refused to obey, neither were mindful of Thy wonders that Thou didst among them; but hardened their necks, and in their rebellion appointed a captain to return to their bondage; but Thou are a God ready to pardon, gracious and merciful, slow to anger, and of great kindness, and forsookest them not. Yea, when they had made them a molten calf, and said, This is thy God that brought thee up out of gypt and had wrought great provocations; Yet Thou in thy manifold mercies forsookest them not in the wilderness; the pillar of the cloud departed not from them by day, to lead them in the way; neither the pillar of fire by night, to show them light, and the way wherein they should go.

- Nehemiah 9:16-19

How!?! That is probably the first question one asks when he reads of Israel's obstinate rebellion in the face of God. It's one thing to rebel against one whom you know is watching you and set the rules for you, but it's another to rebel against the one who lovingly cares for you and supplies ALL your needs! God was both the commander and caretaker of Israel. He gave them His word and did wonders among them to care for them. They, however, denied His presence and provision and rejected His holiness and mercy. They refused to obey His holy laws and blinded themselves to the merciful wonders He did for them. Thus and instead, they created their god to be among them and - being that it couldn't provide for them - longed and planned to return to the harsh slavery of Egypt so they could eat.

And are we today not the same as they. We sin too. Think of what needs to be done in order for one to sin. 1) With the heavens and our own being crying of God, we must deny His presence - or who He is - that we may justify our rebellion. 2) We must refuse to acknowledge that God cares for us. This leads to obstinate rebellion - thus and instead of enjoying God's presence and provision - which may come with some affliction - we usurp God with self and long to return to sin's bondage so our flesh can be satisfied for a season - for its not eternal satisfaction.

But God is ready to pardon, gracious and merciful, slow to anger and of great kindness. This shouldn't prompt us to sin but obey out of love. And of past sins, this shouldn't keep us from God but draw us to Him that He may forgive us. Only rejection of accepting God's pardon keeps us from Him!!!!

Thou gavest also Thy good spirit to instruct them, and withheldest not hy manna from their mouth, and gavest them water for their thirst. Yea, forty years didst Thou sustain them in the wilderness, so that they lacked nothing; their clothes waxed not old, and their feet swelled not. Moreover Thou gavest them kingdoms and nations, and didst divide them into corners: so they possessed the land of Sihon, and the land of the king of Heshbon, and the land of Og king of Bashan. Their children also multipliedst Thou as the stars of heaven, and broughtest them into the land concerning which Thou hadst promised to their fathers, that they should go in to possess it.

- Nehemiah 9:20-23

Contentment: this is something most difficult to develop but most valuable when had. It is our nature to want more, not to be satisfied. We even have spiffy sayings for our greed: "The grass is always greener on the other side of the fence." Ecclesiastes 1:8 sates, "the eye is not satisfied with seeing, nor the ear filled with hearing." Adam and Eve living in perfection were no different; they wanted to be like God, ate the forbidden fruit, and cast all humanity in sin. Israel was no different. God gave them guidance, food and water, clothes that didn't wear out, health, victory over enemies, lands and large families. They lacked NOTHING, and still they wanted more!

We are no different than they, but we can be. We can choose to be content -Yes, contentment is a choice, but it cannot begin there. It doesn't begin in ourselves - remember our nature; so no matter how hard we try on our own, we will never reach contentment. Contentment thus must come from outside man and this world; it can only come from God. Contentment is an available choice only to those who have repented of sin and believed in Christ's sacrifice for them because it is only in Christ. True satisfaction is NOT having all you want, it is realizing you have more than all you need or can imagine. It isn't what one has but who one has. Paul realized this and said, "I have learned in whatever state I am in to be content." We can too! Christ said "Be content... I will never leave or forsake you." Praise God!!!!

So the children went in and possessed the land, and Thou subduedst before them the inhabitants of the land, the Canaanites, and gavest them into their hands, with their kings, and the people of the land, that they might do with them as they would. And they took strong cities and a fat land, and possessed houses full of all goods, wells digged, vineyards, and olive yards, and fruit trees in abundance: so they did eat, and were filled, and became fat, and delighted themselves in Thy great goodness. - Nehemiah 9:24-25

What rich blessings God bestowed on Israel. They entered the Promised Land, and He conquered the inhabitants for them. The city of great fortification, Jericho, trembled and had just reason to fear when Israel approached.

God brought down their mighty walls with only shouting and blowing of trumpets. Not a single Israelite perished though the fledgling army faced warrior nations! As long as they obeyed God, He conquered for them. Even the giants which struck such great fear into their fathers causing them not to enter the land 40 years ago, even those were struck down and driven out of the land. Thus, as God promised, He gave them the land flowing with milk and honey. They delighted themselves in God's great goodness.

We may not face warrior nations in our lives or enter a land of milk and honey, but the command from God is the same for us and the outcome is just as - if not more so - glorious. Every day a child of God faces an enemy more powerful than all flesh and blood: this enemy is sin. God, however and through the blood of His Son, gives us ultimate victory over sin so that we can have victory over it in our every day lives. The only thing we must do - as any soldier should - is obey. That's all Israel did, and that's all we must do. Then we will have victory and enter a position in which we too will be abundantly blessed. With every victory, more blessings come; peace, joy, contentment, etc...: these blessings can fill our spirits even when circumstances are at their worst. So, obey God, claim His victory, and delight yourself in God's great goodness!!!!

Nevertheless they were disobedient, and rebelled against Thee, and cast Thy law behind their backs, and slew Thy prophets which testified against them to turn them to Thee, and they wrought great provocations.
- Nehemiah 9:26

"It is easier for a camel to go through the eye of the needle than for a rich man to enter the kingdom of Heaven," Jesus said to His disciples after being rejected by a rich man. This astonished them, for they believed the rich - of all people - would be in Heaven. Sadly, many who have abundance tend to depend on self and supplies rather than the Savior who gave Himself. It's an easy trap and even the children of God can fall into it. Even though they are eternally saved, they can get so entangled with wealth that they waste their lives with it and do all manner of evil. "The love of money is the root of all evil", Paul warned Timothy.

This is what happened to Israel. God brought them to live in the land of abundance and they began focusing, priding and depending on it. They focused on the blessings without crediting the One who provided the blessing. This caused them to turn instead to false gods; and while they outwardly may have worshipped God, their hearts were blind toward Him. Therefore, they were disobedient to Him obeying instead the wills of their flesh. They rebelled and unified themselves with Satan. Anyone whom God sent to turn them back to Himself, they murdered. They did that which angered God, and God's judgment - as forewarned - burned against them.

Abundance - or desire for it - is not a bad thing. God desires to abundantly bless us and wants us to continually long for Him and His blessings. This, thankfully, is for the purpose of glorifying Him. The best blessings (faith, hope and love) are free and should be sought without reserve! Let us continually enjoy the blessings of God! Proverbs 30:7-9!!!!

Therefore Thou deliveredst them into the hand of their enemies, who vexed them: and in the time of their trouble, when they cried unto Thee, Thou heardest them from heaven; and according to Thy manifold mercies Thou gavest them saviors, who saved them out of the hand of their enemies.
- Nehemiah 9:27

"Whom the LORD loves He chasteneth, and scourgeth every son whom He receiveth...that we might be partakers of this holiness. Now no chastening for the present seemeth to be joyous, but grievous: nevertheless afterward it yielded the peaceable fruit of righteousness unto them which are exercised thereby." Hebrews 12:6, 10b-11.

After repeated warnings and the deaths of many prophets, God disciplined His nation. This may - and does to today's world - seem cruel, but it was done solely out of mercy and love. During such a time in Israel, every man was doing that which was right in his own eyes; the nation was replete with all manner of wickedness and they were living no differently than the idolatrous people around them. This caused much death, pain and suffering. To escape this, they had to forsake their sin and live by God's law. They, however, continued to rebel and wallow in evil. So, to save them from their self-destruction, God punished them. They wanted to live without Him, so He let them.

Then they cried to Him, and He heard them. In His mercy, He forgave and delivered them. He did not leave them though they left Him. He remained faithful to them and ready to pardon.

God hasn't changed; He is the same for us. To those who haven't repented of sin and believed in Christ, He in His mercy draws them to Himself. Those of us who are His children receive discipline when we stray, but it is only for our profit. It is done out of His love; He doesn't enjoy punishing us and this is proven by His immediate forgiveness when we ask. He wants us to repent that He can forgive us and we live for Him and be blessed. Thank God for His enduring forgiving love and mercy!!!!

But after they had rest, they did evil again before Thee; therefore leftest thou them in the hand of their enemies, so that they had the dominion over them; yet when they returned, and cried unto Thee, Thou heardest them from heaven; and many times didst Thou deliver them according to Thy mercies; And testifiedst against them, that Thou mightest bring them again unto Thy law: yet they dealt proudly, and hearkened not unto Thy commandments, but sinned against Thy judgments, (which if a man do, he shall live with them;) and withdrew the shoulder and hardened their neck, and would not hear. Yet many years didst Thou forbear them, and testifiedst against them by the spirit in Thy prophets: yet would they not give ear: therefore gavest Thou them into the hand of the people of the lands. Nevertheless for Thy great mercies' sake Thou didst not utterly consume them, nor forsake them; for Thou are a gracious and merciful God.   - Nehemiah 9:28-31

Familiar? That's because it is! It sounds repetitive because it was. Israel would rebel; God would rebuke; Israel repented; God restored: this was the cycle Israel repeated. God knew once He forgave and restored them they would rebel again; it was not a surprise to God. He's omniscience, knows ALL. When God sent His prophets to warn Israel, He told them that they would be by all persecuted, hated and rejected because of the message they spoke; they would even be brutally killed! Still God sent them, and still they went. God told them Israel's eyes were blind to the truth and their ears deaf to it because they hated it. Still God sent, and when Isaiah asked how long he should preach when no one listens, God answered - not a day or year - until....until it came to pass, which for him was his life: he was sewn asunder. God is not willing that any should perish in sin, but that all should repent. Of His mercy the weeping prophet Jeremiah, who also lived during Israel's rebellion, stated, "Your mercies are new every morning." When we find ourselves sinning again, we can know that God is merciful. He will let us know His mercy until it's too late for us. He is always willing to forgive. His mercies are new every day!!!!

Now therefore, our God, the great the mighty, and the terrible God, who keepest covenant and mercy, let not all the trouble seem little before Thee, that hath come upon us, on our kings, on our princes, and on our priests, and on our prophets, and on our fathers, and on all Thy people, since the time of the kings of Assyria unto this day. - Nehemiah 9:32

After recounting their past sins and God's mercy - and why they were where they were - Israel called on God to notice them. It wasn't that they thought God had forgotten them; they wanted God to do something about their troubles as He so mercifully had done in the past. They were home but under harsh Persian rule and taxes, so they called upon Him on that basis. Asaph in Psalm 77 was greatly troubled and thought God had left Him, but then he recalled God's deliverance of Israel at the Red Sea. He cleaved to that truth and rested in the assurance that God would lead him too. We too can have hope and thus peace even in the midst of our most difficult days; we can by remembering God's past mercies and relying on His present love by calling to Him and trusting in Him to take care of it.

Israel laid their troubles before God and asked Him "let not all our trouble seem small before Thee." Though their calamity covered all of them, from the highest to the holiest to the lowliest, and though this trial extended well over 70 years, they realized that it was small when compared to God and His dealings. He wields the world according to His will; what is our life much less trials when compared to Him! Still He desires us to pour our hearts out to Him, and He promises to take care of it - all of it- and to work it all out for good if we trust Him. In the end, we will be more like Christ and God will receive the glory. Praise God for His love and care throughout all time!!!!

Howbeit Thou art just in all that is brought upon us; for Thou has done right, but we have done wickedly: Neither have our kings, our princes, our priests, nor our fathers, kept Thy law, nor hearkened unto Thy commandments and Thy testimonies, wherewith Thou didst testify against them. For hey have not served Thee in their kingdom, and in Thy great goodness that Thou gavest them, and in the large and fat land Thou gavest before them, neither turned they from their wicked works.   - Nehemiah 9:33-35

Here we see a mark of true repentance. Yes, Israel's present condition was due to their disobedience; and yes, they were asking God to deliver them. However, even in the midst of their punishment, they acknowledged and announced that God was just in His judging of them. He had done right to them at all times, but they had repaid His blessings with heinous rebellion. This stiff-necked pride extended throughout the land on all people for they had all stopped their ears and was incorrigible. Thus, in their prayer of repentance and plea for restoration, they made a proclamation of God's righteousness. God had done right, continued to do right and would forever do right. Israel was truly repentant for they saw their sin as God does and humbly accepted their punishment.

Why do we repent? Do we have true repentance or is it superficial? All of this is determined by our view of God. If we see God as one who excuses sin, we won't see a need to repent. We, however, know that God cannot look favorably upon sin but must judge it. Do we see God as one who can be pacified into forgiving us our sins? Israel did at one time and the result was more evil. They did all that was outwardly possible in their repentance, but their hearts were not repentant. They only "repented" to get God to stop punishing them; they had no acceptance of their sins and God's justice in punishing them. This made a gumball-machine mentality: I put enough into God, and He'll give me what I want. WICKED THOUGHT! Do we see God as righteous, full of mercy and loving? He is, and a true view of God leads one to true repentance: we're wicked; but, God, You're right!!!!

Behold, we are servants this day, and for the land that Thou gavest unto our fathers to eat the fruit thereof and the good thereof, behold, we are servants in it: And it yielded much increase unto the kings whom Thou hast set over us because of our sins: also, they have dominion over our bodies, and over our cattle, at their pleasure, and we are in great distress. And because of all this we make a sure covenant, and writ it; and our princes, Levites, and priests, seal unto it. - Nehemiah 9:36-38

In their prayer to God, Israel had humbly recognized that they were sinners before God, that their past was littered with sin and that through it all God was just and merciful ready to pardon and bless all repentant people. This led them to the conclusion and thus resolution of their prayer: they did not - by any means or for any reason - belong to themselves; they either served sin unto death or God unto life. They didn't deny the extreme distress they were suffering, so much so, that they and theirs belonged to the Persians. They had concluded that it was just; and despite all they ultimately were God's which, even in suffering, is better than belonging to sin. Therefore, they made a resolution, a covenant with God, to obey God not only individually but as a nation. This was a serious, permanent thing that would hold them accountable for all generations.

This conclusion and covenant should be one for every person on Earth, especially a child of God. In light of our past, our own sinfulness, and God's unfailing mercy, we should come humbly before Him and long whole-heartedly to do His commands. We belong to Him or to sin, so let us be His servants, eager to keep and carry out His every desire with clarity. Let us review our own lives, recognize God's love and mercy in them, and resolve to obey Him." Remember thy creator...fear God and keep His commandments for this is the whole duty of man." Ecclesiastes 12:1,13!!!!

SMILE!!! SCRIPTURE STUDIES: NEHEMIAH

Now those that sealed were, Nehemiah, the Tirshatha, the son of Hachaliah, and Zidkijah, Seraiah, Azariah, Jeremiah, Pashur, Amariah, Malchijah, Hattush, Shebaniah, Malluch, Harim, Meremoth, Obadiah, Daniel, Ginnethon, Baruch, Meshullam, Abijah, son of Azaniah, Binnui of the sons of Henadad, Kadmiel; and their brethren, Shebaniah, Hodijah, Kelita, Pelaiah, Hana, Micha, Rehob, Hashabiah, Zaccur, Sherebiah, Shebaniah, Hodijah, Bani, Beninu. The chief of the people; Parosh, Pahathmoab, Elam, Zatthu, Bani, Bunni, Azgad, Bebai, Hariph, Anathoth, Nebai, Magpiah, Meshullam, Hezie, Meshezabeel, Zadok, Jaddua, Pelatiah, Hana, Anaiah, Hoshea, Hananiah, Hashub, Hallohesh, Pileha, Shobek, Rehum, Hashabnah, Maaseiah, and Ahijan, Hanan, Anan, Malluck, Harim, Baanah. - Nehemiah 10:1-27

Eighty four -- that's how many names sealed the covenant. Now, how many of those can you name from memory? Most of us probably can't remember very many. This isn't a bad thing, but it does prove one thing: these names are just that, they're merely names to us with no significance of meaning, except maybe Nehemiah. Each of these names, however, is a person like you and me with feelings, families and friends. They had a past, present and future with joys and sorrows.

Each one made a sacrifice in sealing that covenant. Covenants were cut because they involved an animal sacrifice. These men also sacrificed their own fleshly desires that they might do God's will. They sacrificed having a life unto themselves. Signing the covenant meant setting their lives out on display as an example of that covenant to everyone. These men were not only responsible for self but their entire family. They had to maintain God's law individually and in their families. They were willing. They weren't super or more holy than any one of us. They were men, but they chose to be God's men.

Read this line again: Anan, Malluch, Harim, Baanah, _____ (your name). Would you want that? Exchange the names with those whom you know and love. It means more now doesn't it? Keep it that way! Consider it for a time. This is how it should be. Live that way!!!!

And the rest of the people, the priest, the Levites, the porters, the singers, the Nethinim, and all they that had separated themselves from the people of the lands unto the law of God, their wives, their sons, and their daughters, every one having knowledge, and having understanding. They clave to their brethren, their nobles, and entered into a curse, and into an oath, to walk in God's law, which was given by Moses the servant of God, and to observe and do all the commandments of the LORD our Lord, and His judgments and His statutes. - Nehemiah 10:28-29

This is the response of those who did not put their name to seal. They too entered into a covenant, and while this covenant's focus and purpose was between God and each individual, it was also between man and man to hold each other accountable. When one repents of sin and believes in Christ, he is made a child of God. This eternal, blessed relationship is between God and the individual. However, this isn't the only relationship he enters; he enters into a relationship with other children of God as a brother or sister in Christ. He is now accountable not only to God - as all men are - but to his spiritual siblings; he also becomes responsible for their spiritual condition. This accountability and responsibility is stronger and greater than that between those of the world. Theirs is by physical birth and based on their own hearts which naturally and normally seek for self betterment; their relationship is also temporal; it lasts only as long as their physical existence, for those without Christ die and open their eyes in the torments of Hell where they will forever suffer alone from God and man. A child of God enters that relationship by choice, the choice to repent of sin and believe in Christ. This relationship is thus by spiritual birth, based on the holy, merciful heart of God, and eternal for at death he lives in Heaven with God and his spiritual family. Therefore, his life on earth is to be one of God's love seeking the betterment of all men especially his spiritual siblings. He is to lovingly warn them when they stray from God and accept warning when he strays; he is to encourage and help them do God's will, and he is to pray for them.

What a blessed relationship a child of God has not only with God but with his spiritual family!!!!

They clave to their brethren, their nobles, and entered into a curse, and into an oath, to walk in God's law, which was given by Moses the servant of God, and to observe and do all the commandments of the LORD our Lord, and His judgments and His statues. - Nehemiah 10:29

The people entered into a covenant with God. When they did, they promised to accept both the blessings and curses/punishments from God. Too many of us, as God's children, want the blessings that come from the relationship, but we don't want the discipline that comes after our rebellion. This, however, can't and shouldn't be. Left to ourselves, we reach every depth of depravity; our hearts are desperately wicked. We need the discipline of God. It is a blessing. As Hebrews clarifies "it is for our profit, that we may be partakers of His holiness". It is God's love; for whom He loves, He chastens, that means teaches, which at times requires discipline. Let us not mock, despise or reject His discipline; but let us thank Him for it and heed to it. Let us be glad He doesn't leave or forsake us to waste our lives in sin.

God's blessings aren't just limited to discipline. He also blesses us with peace, joy, love, contentment, hope, etc... Remember, however, though God supplies these in abundance, we must accept them. Who wouldn't?! We don't always. Instead of peace, we worry; instead of joy, we complain and pity our selves; we always can find something negative to rob us of God's blessings. God still offers them to us, and we need only trust Him and obey Him to receive them. We who have repented and believed are God's. How blessed we are!!!!

And that we should not give our daughters unto the people of the land, nor take their daughter for our sons. - Nehemiah 10:30

Israel made a covenant with God, and now they begin to specify certain things they would no longer do, things that caused God's discipline in the first place. The first thing they mentioned was that they would be faithful to God in their marriages. This was a time when parents chose the spouses of their children, so the parents promised to no longer marry their children to the peoples of the land. This was a command of God from the very beginning. It wasn't because God was prejudiced and hated other people. It was because other people hated God and sought false gods to worship. By giving their children to marry those who weren't God fearing, they condoned false gods and put their children in relationships that would lead them from God to false gods. When this happened, families would turn to idolatry and, like a disease, soon the nation would turn to idolatry for what is a nation but its families. This happened to Israel in their past and, sadly, again in their future. Both times they incurred God's punishment upon them.

Marriage is the first institution of God: He made man and woman. It is more than just a relationship; it is the most important, vital covenant a man and woman can make for it begins a family, and families create a nation. Therefore, it is essential that both the man and woman put God first and love - not each other - but God most; God teaches us how to love each other the way we should. A marriage needs to be three: God, man and woman. The foundation should be God because His love is stronger than any human affection or circumstance. A marriage where one is God fearing but the other isn't is difficult; and though God can use the Godly spouse to win the other to Him, one should never enter into such a covenant willingly with an unbeliever. Always be faithful to God both before and during marriage. He made it, and He will sustain it!!!!

And if the people of the land bring ware or any victuals on the Sabbath day to sell, that we would not buy it of them on the Sabbath, or on the holy day: and that we would leave the seventh year, and the exaction of every debt. - Nehemiah 10:31

Under Old Testament law, Israel was not to do any work on the Sabbath. This was because God finished and thus ceased from creating on the seventh day; He set it apart by deed and command as a day of rest, holy unto Him. When Israel broke this law, they showed to the other nations a lack of faith in and disrespect for God. A similar law to this was known as the Year of Jubilee, a year every seventh year wherein Israel was to forgive all debts, return all lands to the original owners and not work the land but let it rest and glean from what it brought forth naturally. Israel, however, hadn't kept this command, and for 49 years - 7 Jubilees - they worked the land and didn't release their fellow Israelites from debt. This was the reason they spent 49 years in captivity when God disciplined them.

Israel lacked faith in believing God would care for them when they obeyed; they also loved money. This led to their disobedience and thus God's discipline. Had they trusted God to provide, they would have obeyed Him and not so frantically and futilely depended on themselves to provide. Had they not loved money, they would have obeyed and not robbed God of His day to make a little extra pay.

We, today, are no longer under Old Testament law, but its principles remain for all time and for us. We do not have Sabbath, but we do have a Lord's Day, a day set apart for the worship of God. We do not have a year of Jubilee, but its principle remains too. Fear God and keep His commandments; love the Lord our God with all your heart, soul and mind and love your neighbor as yourself. Do not lack faith or love money. Conduct all your business dealings toward the honor and glory of God - no cheating, lying or stealing. Trust God to provide for you - He promised He would - and obey Him in all your workings and with all your material possessions!!!!

Also, we made ordinances for us, to charge ourselves yearly with the third part of a shekel for the service of the house of our God; For the showbread, and for the continual meat offering, of the Sabbaths, of the new moons, for the set feasts, and for the holy things, and for the sin offerings to make an atonement of Israel, and for all the work of the house of our God. And we cast the lots among the priests, the Levites, and the people, for the wood offering, to bring it into the house of our God, after the houses of our fathers, at times appointed year by year, to burn upon the altar of the LORD our God, as it is written in the law. - Nehemiah 10:32-34

    Israel's third part dealt with the care of the worship of God. They had dedicated to God the marriages of their sons and daughters and their business dealings to God; now they dedicated their money to the care of God's worship. They wanted to honor and glorify God not with just how they made money but with how they spent money. Therefore, they made a yearly tax which was to be used for the upkeep of the service, and they began a rotation for the people to bring wood for the sacrifices at the temple. They understood that the best way to take care of their money was to give to the Lord. If they took care of the service of the Lord, He would take care of them so they could continue taking care of it.

    We too need to dedicate our money to honoring and glorifying God. There is nothing better we can do with it! Furthermore, God already promised to take care of all our needs, so we have no reason to hoard away our money and not freely, cheerfully give it to Him. When we give to God, it opens the door for God to use that money in ways we could never imagine and for purposes far greater than we could accomplish by keeping it and with effects that last for eternity. We can never do that with it!

    Another reason to liberally give to God is because He freely gave His Son, Christ, to die for us that we by repentance and faith may have eternal life with Him and not die. Let us give for He first gave to us!!!!

And to bring the first fruits of our ground, and the first fruits of all fruit of all trees, year by year, unto the house of our God: And that we should bring the first fruits of our dough, and our offerings, and the fruit of all manner of trees, of wine and of oil, unto the priests, to the chambers of the house of our God; and the tithes of our ground unto the Levites, that the same Levites might have the tithes in all the cities of our tillage. And the priest the son of Aaron shall be with the Levites, when the Levites take tithes: and the Levites shall bring up the tithe of the tithes unto the house of our God, to the chambers, into the treasure house. For the children of Israel and the children of Levi shall bring the offering of the corn, of the new wine, and the oil, unto the vessels of the sanctuary, and the priests that minister, and the porters, and the singers: and we will not forsake the house of our God.
- Nehemiah 10:35-39

Israel promised to care for the service of God, now they also promised to care for the servants of the worship of God. The tribe of Levi was the only tribe out of the 12 who didn't receive an inheritance in the Promised Land. Instead, they were given the cities of refuge throughout the land, and they were to be provided for by the other tribes. This was because they were set apart for the service of God. Thus Israel promised to resume caring for the Levites and priests as they should.

The Levites, however, were not exempt from tithing. Everyone had to tithe the first part of all they gained or had. The rest was to care for their family. It took faith to do this; the crop may be small, the cows may only calf once, but Israel trusted God to take care of them.

"Where your treasure is your heart will be also...you cannot serve God and mammon", Jesus warned. If your heart is set on money or even family, you will serve it and not give it to the Lord. If you heart, however, is set on God, you won't have trouble giving to Him to care for His servants and service. Your willingness to give to God is a direct reflection of where your heart is, whom you serve. Trust and serve God!!!!

And the rulers of the people dwelt at Jerusalem: the rest of the people also cast lots, to bring one of the ten to dwell in Jerusalem the holy city, and nine parts to dwell in other cities. And the people blessed all the men, that willingly offered themselves to dwell at Jerusalem. - Nehemiah 11:1-2

What is a city - even the most beautiful and fortified city - without inhabitants?! It is a ghost town and easily vulnerable to destruction from time and enemies. Thus Jerusalem needed dwellers, but these dwellers had to be brave pioneers for they faced many changes and difficulties. Therefore, the first to go were the leaders to lead by example as it should be. Then the people agreed to let 1 of every 10 go to Jerusalem. Lastly, men volunteered to go and received a special blessing for doing so. These families gave up lands, houses, businesses, and families. They didn't do it to gain anything immediately better but to start completely over with nothing, to struggle to make a life and city prosperous. They became targets for attacks. If the enemies threatened attack even before the wall was built, they probably really wanted to attack now that it was being inhabited! Still these people trusted God to provide for and protect them.

As Psalm 23 states, "Thou leadeth me in the paths of righteousness for Thy name's sake. Yea, though I walk through the valley of the shadow of death, I will fear no evil: for Thou art with me." The path of righteousness isn't always the easiest to take- and in fact is promised to be difficult. It takes faith for at times it leads through dangers and difficulties, but we have nothing to fear for even then it is the safest place to be because God is with us. Because of Him whether dangers surrounds us or not our cup runneth over with blessings, and we peacefully rest knowing that He maketh us to dwell in safety and to dwell in the house of the Lord forever. Where God leads us, we need never worry or fear but walk boldly in His steps and trust confidently in who He is as the one who goes before us, supplies for and protects us!!!!

All the sons of Perez that dwelt at Jerusalem were four hundred threescore and eight valiant men. And after him Gabbai, Sallai, nine hundred twenty and eight. Seraiah the son of Hilkiah, the son of Meshullam, the son of Zadok, the son of Ahitub, was the ruler of the house of God. And the brethren that did the work of the house were eight hundred twenty and two: and Adaiah the son of Jeroham, the son of Pelaliah, the son of Amzi, the son of Zechariah the son of Pashu, the son of Malchiah, and his brethren, chief of the fathers, two hundred forty and two: and Amashai the son of Azareel, the son of Ahasai, the son of Meshillemoth, the son of Immer, and their brethren mighty men of valor; a hundred twenty and eight: and their overseer was Zadbiel, the son of one of the great men. Also of the Levites: Shemaiah the son of Hashub, the son of Azrikam, the son of Hashabiah, the son of Bunni: and Shabbethai and Jozabad, of the chief of the Levites, had the oversight of the outward business of the house of God. And Mattaniah the son of Micha, the son of Zabdi, the son of Asaph, was the principal to begin the thanksgiving in prayer: and Bakbukiah the second among his brethren, and Adba the son of Shammua, the son of Galal, the son of Jeduthun. All the Levites in the holy city were two hundred fourscore and four. Moreover the porters, Akkub, Talmon, and their brethren that kept the gates, were a hundred seventy and two. And the residue of Israel, of the priests, and the Levites, were in all the cities of Judah, every one in his inheritance.

- Nehemiah 11:6, 8, 11-20

These aren't just names and numbers; these are people and families. These are as God recorded them "valiant men, mighty men of valor." Think about it: God all powerful and holy recorded these men as valiant and mighty! What an honor, but let us not forget by whom and for whom these men were courageous. They were only so by God's power. God gave them their strength; so when they were courageous, it was by God. They used it when they did God's will and moved into Jerusalem; hence, it was for God. God is the strength of every one of His own; we have nothing to fear, and the best way to use that limitless courage is doing God's will. The more we use it for God, the more God will give us.

These were also those who had purpose in moving into the city. God did not allow a group of people to inhabit Jerusalem and do the best they could to find purpose for being there. He gave them purpose. Each one had a place to be and a job to fulfill whether it was as a manager or a managed, everyone was responsible for something. No one was left out; every eight, two and four was counted and recorded.

Each of us is important to God. He does not overlook or ignore any one. He has a purpose for each of us; that purpose joins those of others, and each and corporately we honor and glorify God!!!!

But the Nithinim dwelt in Ophel: and Ziha and Gispa were over the Nethinim. The overseer also of the Levites at Jerusalem was Uzzi the son of Bani, the son of Hashabiah, the son of Mattaniah, the son of Micha. Of the sons of Asaph, the singers were over the business of the house of God. For it was the king's commandment concerning them, that a certain portion should be for the singers, due for every day. And Pethahiah the son of Meshezabeel, of the children of Zerah the son of Judah, was at the king's hand in all matters concerning the people. - Nehemiah 11:21-24

Here we find the Nethinims, descendants of the Gibeonites who through trickery formed a pact with Israel and by becoming their slaves saved the Gibeonite people and dwelt among Israel. They now dwelt in Ophel, a city on the wall, so that they may continue to fulfill their pact and perform their duties. Over these people, were Ziha and Gispa.

Over all the Levites in Jerusalem was Uzzi. He had to be sure each priest did his duty. This wasn't just delegation; this was delegation by God's organization. Each priestly family had its own special responsibility given to them by God Himself in Numbers 4. No family was to share in another family's duties. This happened to Uzzah, who while incorrectly transporting the Ark of the Covenant, touched it to stabilize it and was struck dead. Uzzi had a grave responsibility, one that required extensive knowledge of not only how things should be done (which also had many specifications set by God) but who should do them.

Then we have the sons of Asaph who cared for not only the singing but some repairs of the temple as well. The king himself ordered them to be paid for their work. Lastly, in charge of it all, was Pethahiah. He alone answered to the king in ALL things concerning the people; taxes, reports, requests, etc...

Note, though these Jews prayed for deliverance! They didn't rebel but served the Persian king as they should. They waited on God's timing. Things may not be ideal for God's children today, but we should continue to serve God and our country as we should. Obey God, and you will live to your country as you should!!!!

And at the dedication of the wall of Jerusalem they sought the Levites out of all their places, to bring them to Jerusalem, to keep the dedication with gladness, both with thanksgivings, and with singing with cymbals, psalteries, and with harps. And the songs of the singers gathered themselves together, both out of the plain country round about Jerusalem, and from the villages of Netophathi; Also from the house of Gilgal, and out of the fields of Geba and Azmaveth: for the singer had builded them villages round about Jerusalem. And the priest and the Levites purified themselves, and purified the people, and the gates, and the wall. - Nehemiah 12: 27-30

The time had come, now that the wall had been completed and the city inhabited, to dedicate the whole to the Lord. The city Jerusalem and the temple was already holy unto the Lord; it had been so for centuries. Jerusalem held the first, most glorious temple Solomon built. That, however, was destroyed because of Israel's sin and by Nebuchadnezzar when he led them to captivity. So, why the dedication if it already belonged to God? The people's sin of disobedience estranged them from God; that sin also corrupted and polluted the city and temple. Instead of being used for God's honor and glory, they were defiled by their worship to false gods and the passive thus inadequate worship to God! Therefore, both needed to be rededicated to God, starting by purifying them and the people.

All dedication should and must begin with the conviction by the Holy Spirit to do so and then purification. All purification is only by blood, in Old Testament times, it was the sprinkling of an unblemished sacrificed animal. That animal was a picture of Christ. Now that Christ has come and shed His blood, we don't need to look forward to it with a picture of how it will be complete in Christ; we need only repent of sin and believe. Then we are forgiven and dedicated to God. Even though this is eternal, however, our fellowship can be broken by sin. Tragically, some even forget they were saved! Thankfully, God by Christ's blood is ready to forgive, to restore fellowship and allow us to rededicate our lives to Him. It's through His blood!!!!

Then I brought up the princes of Judah upon the wall, and appointed two great companies of them that gave thanks, whereof one went on the right hand upon the wall toward the dung gate: And after them went Hoshaiah, and half of the princes of Judah, ... And the other company of them that gave thanks went over against them, and I after them, and the half of the people upon the wall, from beyond the tower of the furnaces even unto the broad wall; ... So stood the two companies of them that gave thanks in the house of God, and I, and the half of the rulers with me: And the priests; Eliakim, Maaseiah, Miniamin, Michaiah, Elioenai, Zechariah, and Hananiah, with trumpets; And Maaseiah, and Shemaiah, and Eleazar, and Uzzi, and Jehohanan, and Malchijah, and Elam, and Ezer. And the singers sang loud, with Jezrahiah their overseer. Also that day they offered great sacrifices, and rejoiced: for God had made them rejoice with great joy: the wives also and the children rejoiced: so that the joy of Jerusalem was heard even afar off.
 - Nehemiah 12:31-32, 38, 40-43

This dedication was a celebration of much thanksgiving and great joy. Every dedication should contain both silent reverence of a contrite heart before the holy God and joyful praise of the same heart forgiven and ready to begin anew in its service to God. Israel was like this. They gathered the priest, the singers, the musicians, and the people and praised God. They thanked God for His rich blessings and sang loudly because God had given them reason to rejoice with great joy. That reason was a new start.

The joy of Jerusalem was so loud that they were heard afar off by other nations, and their enemies probably heard it too! What a testimony! Their joy was so great others could testify of it! This is the way our joy should be. Others should be able to undoubtedly see our joy. Peter wrote that our joy should be so evident others ask us about it, and this was the case when Paul and Silas were beaten, chained, and cast into the lowest prison. All of the prison rang with their joy. It was such a witness that when an earthquake freed everyone, no one left but asked about their joy, and many were saved. May every Christian's joy be so great!!!!

And at that time were some appointed over the chambers for the treasures, for the offerings, for the firstfruits, and for the tithes, to gather them out of the fields of the cities the portions of the law for the priests and Levites: for Judah rejoiced for the priests and for the Levites that waited. And both the singers and the porters kept the ward of their God, and the ward of the purification, according to the commandment of David, and of Solomon his son. For in the days of David and Asaph of old there were chief of the singers, and songs of praise and thanksgiving unto God. And all Israel in the days of Zerubbabel, and in the days of Nehemiah, gave the portions of the singers and the porters, every day his portion: and they sanctified holy things unto the Levites; and the Levites sanctified them unto the children of Aaron.
- Nehemiah 12:44-47

During the dedication, it was decided that there should be those who went to the cities and gathered from them the portions due to the priest and Levites. These portions were like a tax taken to care for the ministers of the temple; it was commanded by God for two reasons. First, the Levites were sanctified unto God in the place of every first born son in Israel. They were to work solely for God. Second, they did not receive an inheritance in the Promise Land because they were sanctified unto the Lord's work. Therefore, it was the people's responsibility to care for the priest and Levites, and it became the singers' and porters' responsibility to gather and tend to what was given. These individuals also received portions from Israel for their work as commanded by their most respected king, David. And everyone did their work as God commanded.

It is good to give to care for one's pastor who has - like the Levites - dedicated his life to the service of God and thus care for God's people of whom God has charged him. God has commanded it of us. "Don't muzzle the ox while it is treading," 1 Timothy 5:18. A laborer is worth his wages. If he isn't cared for, he won't be able to work as he should. Thus, we must care for our pastors, and - like Judah - rejoice in those who are faithful to God in their work for God!!!!

On that day they read in the book of Moses in the audience of the people; and therein was found written, that the Ammonite and the Moabite should not come into the congregation of God for ever; Because they met not the children of Israel with bread and with water, but hired Balaam against them, that he should curse them: howbeit our God turned the curse into a blessing. Now it came to pass, when they had heard the law, that they separated from Israel all the mixed multitude. - Nehemiah 13:1-3

As the people drew closer to God, they grew more conscience of His commands. This command was a fulfillment of God's promise to Abraham over 1,000 years ago. God said that He would bless those who blessed Israel and curse those who cursed Israel. Though God forbid Balaam to curse Israel and actually turned the curse to a blessing, the Ammonites and Moabites still cursed in their hearts and caused Israel to sin with adultery and idolatry. Hundreds died of the judgment plague God sent. Moab and Ammon were forbidden to dwell with Israel forever. Israel thus removed them from the people. This was not prejudice. Any Ammonite or Moabite who truly desired to be one of God's people could be. They needed only repent of their sin and believe in God's promises; when they did this, they too would obey God's law and live as an Israelite. No longer would they seek and follow the idolatry and the ways of their people. This is proven by Ruth, the Moabitess, who repented, left her people, lived as an Israelite, and became part of Jesus' ancestry! The people who were separated from among Israel were those who chose to continue in the sins of their people; they were those who would lead Israel astray from God.

Our lives and churches today are littered with Ammonites and Moabites, those people who are of the world and thus, like those nations, lead us away from God. They don't announce it, but do it subtly under the cause of evangelism. Slowly they begin to use the ways of the world to attract the people of the world; they say we need to update the Bible and its way of reaching people. This is wrong! If we use the world to attract the world or if we allow the world into our lives so we can show them Christ, we defeat our purpose. The world can't show God; we end up being like the world! We are called to be different, be in the world not of it!!!!

And before this, Eliashib the priest, having the oversight of the chamber of the house of our God, was allied unto Tobiah: And he had prepared for him a great chamber, where aforetime, they laid the meat offerings, the frankincense, and the vessels, and the tithes of the corn, the new wine, and the oil, which was commanded to be given to the Levites, and the singers, and the porters; and the offerings of the priests. But in all this time was not I at Jerusalem: for in the two and thirtieth year of Artaxerxes king of Babylon came I unto the king, and after certain days obtained I leave of the king: - Nehemiah 13:4-6

Sometime after the revivals, Nehemiah had to leave to attend his duties before the king. He was there around 10 years. It was during this time the effects of the revival slowly dissipated, and sadly some returned to their former lives having no true, deep, committed revival in their hearts. This was what happened to the priest Eliashib. He united, or maybe reunited (Nehemiah 6:17-19, some were sworn to him), with Tobiah, the very enemy who tried to prevent the building of the wall, the very ones from whom Israel was to separate themselves, the Ammonites! This wicked union led to Eliashib actually accommodating idolatrous Tobiah in a chamber dedicated to God! This was a great chamber purposed to care for the servants of God. So, Eliashib not only abused his position, he robbed God's servants and ultimately robbed God. Even if he did have "good" intentions, Eliashib did wrong.

Before condemning Eliashib though, let us examine our own lives. Even after acknowledging and repenting of our sin, how often do we reunite with that same sin or unite with a different way of the world? That union is deadly and must be broken to avoid the destruction it will bring. Any union with sin takes the place of God in our hearts, and before long we find ourselves completely submitting to it and making accommodations for it in our lives - sacrificing time, money, and family: many have lost it all to accommodate their addiction to their sin union. It doesn't start that way, but it doesn't take long to get there! Break unions to sin and cleave to God, for none can embrace God AND sin!!!!

And I came to Jerusalem, and understood of the evil that Eliashib did for Tobiah, in preparing him a chamber in the courts of the house of God. And it grieved me sore: therefore I cast forth all the household stuff of Tobiah out of the chamber. Then I commanded, and they cleansed the chambers: and thither brought I again the vessels of the house of God, with the meat offering and the frankincense. - Nehemiah 13:7-9

Like Nehemiah toward Eliashib's wicked union, we need to be sorely grieved at others as well as our own unions with sin. This should cause us to act against such evil, break the unions in our lives, cast out the temptations/instigators of it, and once again sanctify and dedicate our lives to God, filling them with the things of God. By doing this, we can live eternally prosperous lives for God and not waste our lives on the egregious pleasures of the world.

First, we must break our union with sin - whether it is an addiction, relationship, or something else. When we understand by the conviction of the Holy Spirit - for there must be a change toward God - the sin in our lives and the holiness of God, we can repent of that sin, thus breaking our union with it. Repentance is vital; without it, we are still in sin without hope, separated from God. Then we must, and as an effect/proof of repentance, cast out temptations/instigators of that sin. Separate yourself from bad company (Psalm 1:1); trash bad books, movies, etc... This isn't easy, but it is necessary and that is why it's by God's strength we do it. Lastly, we must fill that void with the things of God. Memorize Scripture against that sin, associate with those who will help you avoid sit (Psalms 1:2). If we don't do this, that void will be filled with the things of evil, and you will be worse off having experienced forgiveness but returning to evil. Our hearts will be harder to the conviction of God the more we return to that sin. All of this involves a serious, conscience choice from the sinner. It isn't easy; but in Christ, it is possible because He alone gives us victory over sin, enabling us to live lives for God!!!!

And I perceived that the portions of the Levites had not been given them: for the Levites and the singers, that did the work, were fled every one to his field. Then contended I with the rulers, and said, Why is the house of God forsaken? And I gathered them together, and set them in their place. Then brought all Judah the tithe of the corn and the new wine and the oil unto the treasuries. And I made treasurers over the treasuries, Shelemiah the priest, and Zadok the scribe, and of the Levites, Pedaiah: and next to them was Hanan the son of Zaccur, the son of Mattaniah: for they were counted faithful, and their office was to distribute unto their brethren. Remember me, O my God, concerning this, and wipe not out my good deeds that I have done for the house of my God, and for the offices thereof.
                                                              - Nehemiah 13:10-14

    After casting out Tobiah, Nehemiah perceived that even the people had forsaken their privileged responsibility of giving to support God's servants. As a result, those who were supposed to be dedicated solely to God had to leave their service to work in the fields to provide for their families. This was a tragedy, not only were the people depriving themselves of God's blessings for giving, but of their spiritual warfare in not supplying for the ones whom God provided to care for them! When they weren't cared for, they couldn't give their all or best to caring for the spiritual needs of the people. Nehemiah fixed this and set things right again.

    When we refuse, neglect, or forget to give to God, we become as Israel. We rob not only from God and His servants, but from ourselves. We rob ourselves of God's eternal blessings for giving, and we rob ourselves of our spiritual care. Our pastors have to divide their time, "flee to their fields, in order to care for their families." Thus they aren't as able to care for us as much as they would like. Let us always give to God for the care of His work!!!!

In those days saw I in Judah some treading wine presses on the sabbath, and bringing in sheaves, and lading asses; as also wine, grapes, and figs, and all manner of burdens, which they brought into Jerusalem on the sabbath day: and I testified against them in the day wherein they sold victuals. There dwelt men of Tyre also therein, which brought fish, and all manner of ware, and sold on the sabbath unto the children of Judah, and in Jerusalem. Then I contended with the nobles of Judah, and said unto them, What evil thing is this that ye do, and profane the sabbath day? Did not your fathers thus, and did not our God bring all this evil upon us, and upon this city? yet ye bring more wrath upon Israel by profaning the sabbath.

- Nehemiah 13:15-18

How quickly Israel forgot the covenant they made with God; not one generation passed away to the next before they were once again sinning against God on His holy day! Once again they were doing business on the Sabbath, the day God set aside for them to rest and remember him, the day God commanded them and any one among them to do no work. Now not only were others working, but they too. God said through Paul to Timothy that the love of money is the root of all manner of evil. Indeed, Israel is the sad example of this. Nehemiah, however, rebuked them, reminding them of their covenant and revealing to them that their sin was the cause of the evil they suffered and reprimanding them for bringing more punishment of Israel. They had entered into a covenant to do what God commanded, and they also entered into a curse to accept the punishment for not obeying. How sadly are the judgments of God forgotten. Making the commitment isn't enough; one must follow through with it.

It is easy for us to love money above the Lord. When we work instead of worship and hoard instead of give, we excuse our actions by saying we must do so to live. What we do in reality is forget or don't care about God's law. This is evil. Evil brings only evil and punishment. Remember that! Live as God desires, and He will take care of you!!!!

And it came to pass, that when the gates of Jerusalem began to be dark before the sabbath, I commanded that the gates should be shut, and charged that they should not be opened till after the sabbath: and some of my servants set I at the gates, that there should no burden be brought in on the sabbath day. So the merchants and sellers of all kind of ware lodged without Jerusalem once or twice. Then I testified against them, and said unto them, Why lodge ye about the wall? if ye do so again, I will lay hands on you. From that time forth came they no more on the sabbath. And I commanded the Levites that they should cleanse themselves, and that they should come and keep the gates, to sanctify the sabbath day. Remember me, O my God, concerning this also, and spare me according to the greatness of Thy mercy.

- Nehemiah 13:19-22

    Having seen and rebuked Israel for breaking the Sabbath, Nehemiah set out to make things right. He first just closed the gates and set guards to keep merchants from entering, but then the sellers were persistently camping outside of the gate, tempting people to come out and break God's law, waiting for their opportunity to get inside Jerusalem. At such wicked audacity, Nehemiah became angry and confronted them with harsh threats. This worked; and to ensure it continued, he had the Levites cleanse themselves and keep the gates. Then he prayed that God would "remember"/deal with him according to his zealousness for God and thus have mercy upon him.

    Two things to learn here are: first, just because we "closes the gate" to sin doesn't mean the temptation won't wait outside calling to us, hoping to be allowed back into our lives. It takes strong force to resist continually; it takes God's strength to do so unto success. Second, no matter how zealous one is or what good things he does for God, it is still only by the greatness of God's mercy that we are spared from destruction. God's loving kindness sent Christ to die in payment for our sins, and it's that same unfathomable mercy through Christ to us that allows us to live. Let us therefore live by and for God in all we do!!!!

In those days also saw I Jews that had married wives of Ashdod, of Ammon, and of Moab: And their children spake half in the speech of Ashdod, and could not speak in the Jews' language, but according to the language of each people. And I contended with them, and cursed them, and smote certain of them, and plucked off their hair, and made them swear by God, saying, Ye shall not give your daughters unto their sons, nor take their daughters unto your sons, or for yourselves.   - Nehemiah 13:23-25

Nehemiah returned and found not only that the priest had given a chamber of God's to idolatrous Tobiah, that the workers of God were not being cared for, and that the people had stopped giving, but he found that many of them had married idolatrous people! This was the worst thing they could have done as seen by Nehemiah's immediate and extreme reprimanding. The most intense grief, in Jewish culture, was expressed by smoting one's chest, ripping one's coat, and pulling/cutting one's hair. Nehemiah was rebuking them and telling them that their actions should cause intense grief among them. He "cursed them", told them, and was calling down judgment on them. He "smote them" and "plucked off their hair.": If they weren't going to repent on their own, he was going to cause them to do so. This was no polite, sweet request; this was a command.

Why was he so harsh? Notice what he first saw. The people had married idolatrous people and their children were being raised without knowledge or care about God and His Word. They could not even speak the Jewish language! How could they come to know God if they could not even understand the language in which His Word was written!? Their idolatrous parents wouldn't tell them. Their children and grandchildren would continue away from God until the nation was once again lost to idolatry and doomed to God's judgment again.

What a terrible price we pay when we willfully marry people of the world who stand against God. Our children suffer the most being raised in a mixed home at best. They - as we sinners are - are inclined to go the way of the world; they live and raise children the same. This should cause great grief in our hearts and then repentance. Then we should pray for our spouses, children, and families. God can change them too!!!!

Did not Solomon king of Israel sin by these things? yet among many nations was there no king like him, who was beloved of his God, and God made him king over all Israel: nevertheless even him did outlandish women cause to sin. Shall we then hearken unto you to do all this great evil, to transgress against our God in marrying strange wives? - Nehemiah 13:26-27

Nehemiah's upbraiding of the Israelites who married idolatrous people ended by his giving them an example lest they believe themselves beyond the influence of their spouses. "Well," they may rebuttal, "MY spouse doesn't try to influence me toward idols; we each do our own thing. We have no kids and are happy as we are." OR they may have thought, "I married one who doesn't believe as I in the one true God, but I'm too strong to change beliefs; I would never do that." OR maybe even, "I worship with my spouse and my spouse does so with me. If I hadn't married, my spouse wouldn't have even heard about, much less come to, the worship of the true God. This is the only way to convert my spouse." "I did so to help." There are soooo many reasons, excuses, and attempts of justification, but Nehemiah quiets them all.

King Solomon, son of David who was a man after God's own heart: there was no more loved king than he. He was, by the blessing of God, the wisest man ever. He built the unsurpassed in beauty temple of God, and he ruled in peace all the days of his life. No king but his father was revered more, and no man was/is/or will be wiser. YET, even he was led astray to idols by his wives whom he married in the name of peace contracts. Even the wisest man on Earth was influenced away from God after all God did for him and all he did for God! "If he could fall, so can you," Nehemiah silenced them.

"Wherefore" 1 Corinthians 10:12 reads, "let him that thinketh he standeth take heed lest he fall." No one is beyond temptation/influence, and we all are only one yes away from any sin. None is safe; and if he believes he is, he is prideful, and pride leads to destruction. The wisest man on Earth fell, how much more able are we! Thus, one must be careful whom he marries; and if one is already married to an unbeliever, pray hard for them AND themselves that he/she may stand for God and live in such a way that the unbeliever may repent, believe, and then live for God!!!!

And one of the sons of Joiada, the son of Eliashib the high priest, was son in law to Sanballat the Horonite: therefore I chased him from me. Remember them, O my God, because they have defiled the priesthood, and the covenant of the priesthood, and of the Levites. Thus cleansed I them from all strangers, and appointed the wards of the priests and the Levites, every one in his business; And for the wood offering, at times appointed, and for the firstfruits. Remember me, O my God, for good.

- Nehemiah 13:28-31

Not only had Eliashib made a union with Tobiah, giving him a chamber in God's temple, but he also made a union with the other main enemy Sanballat; Eliashib's grandson was married to Sanballat's daughter! Eliashib taught his son the lie that it is good to make unions with the people of the world - especially those in power. His son Joiada (as most children do) then took it a step further and chose Sanballat's daughter to marry his son. They defiled the priesthood and their covenant to remain sanctified to God. Thus Nehemiah chased him out of his office because he would not repent and cleansed the whole of all idolatrous people. When the leaders sin, the people follow. Nehemiah knew this and set things right once again, calling upon God to judge the unfaithful priest who refused to repent.

The last words of the book of Nehemiah are his brief but beautiful prayer to God: "Remember me, O my God, for good." He pleaded for God's blessings as he had done throughout this book and his whole life. Through his sorrows, struggles, and celebrations, Nehemiah is found praying. His life is characterized by prayer, and it was his constant dependence on God that enabled him to endure and achieve victory in all his doings for God. In contrast to those who were born into positions to lead - the priest - but failed due to their unions with sin, Nehemiah became a leader and succeeded because of his union with God.

Everyone is an example/leader to someone. What kind of leader you are depends on with whom you unite. Depend on God; be a strong leader that leads to the victory we have only in God!!!!

Author Bio:

Rachel Wirges-Lott was born the fourth of six children to Robert and Nelwyn Wirges on September 8, 1986, but she is quick to say that isn't as important as her birth into God's family she had later when she repented of sin and trusted in Christ as her Savior. Since then, she with her mother and sisters Laura and Stephanie attended the LR Missionary Baptist Seminary. She, Nelwyn, and Laura received with honors a masters degree in Bible Languages. She teaches with her sister Melissa and her mother at NLR Missionary Baptist where her Dad serves as pastor. She with her husband Samuel are assistant music directors. She also enjoys serving as music directors with her brothers Robert and Stephen at Budd Creek camp.

Rachel and Samuel are blessed with one boy, James Cristofori. Their purpose and prayer is that one day they will see Christ smile and say,

"Well done."

RACHEL WIRGES-LOTT